MW00776314

DEEPENING
LIFE
TOGETHER

ACTS

LIFE TOGETHER

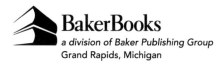

a division of Baker Publishing Group
Grand Rapids, Michigan

© 2009 by Lifetogether Publishing

Published by Baker Books
a division of Baker Publishing Group
P.O. Box 6287, Grand Rapids, MI 49516-6287
www.bakerbooks.com

Printed in the United States of America

Library of Congress Cataloging-in-Publication Data
Acts / [editors, Mark L. Strauss, Teresa Haymaker].
    p.   cm. — (Deepening life together)
   Includes bibliographical references.
   ISBN 978-0-8010-6842-3 (pbk.)
    1. Bible. N.T. Acts—Textbooks. 2. Bible. N.T. Acts—Study and teaching. I. Strauss, Mark L. II. Haymaker, Teresa.
BV2626.A28 2009
226.6′0071—dc22   2009014244

CONTENTS

Contents

ACKNOWLEDGMENTS

The *Deepening Life Together: Acts* Small Group Video Bible Study has come together through the efforts of many at Baker Publishing Group, Lifetogether Publishing, and Lamplighter Media for which we express our heartfelt thanks.

Executive Producer	John Nill
Producer and Director	Sue Doc Ross
Editors	Mark L. Strauss (Scholar), Teresa Haymaker
Curriculum Development	Stephanie French, Teresa Haymaker, Virgil Hurley, Mark L. Strauss, Karen Lee-Thorp
Video Production	Chris Balish, Rodney Bissell, Nick Calabrese, Sebastian Hoppe Fuentes, Josh Greene, Patrick Griffin, Teresa Haymaker, Oziel Jabin Ibarra, Natali Ibarra, Janae Janik, Keith Sorrell, Lance Tracy
Teachers and Scholars	Clint Arnold, Lynn Cohick, Jon Laansma, Nick Perrin, Ben Shin, Mark Strauss, Erik Thoennes
Baker Publishing Group	Jack Kuhatschek

Special thanks to DeLisa Ivy, Bethel Seminary, Talbot School of Theology, Wheaton College

Interior icons by Tom Clark

READ ME FIRST

Most people want to live a healthy, balanced spiritual life, but few achieve this by themselves. And most small groups struggle to balance all of God's purposes in their meetings. Groups tend to overemphasize one of the five purposes, perhaps fellowship or discipleship. Rarely is there a healthy balance that includes evangelism, ministry, and worship. That's why we've included all of these elements in this study so you can live a healthy, balanced spiritual life over time.

A typical group session will include the following:

Memory Verses

For each session we have provided a memory verse that emphasizes an important truth from the session. This is an optional exercise, but we believe that memorizing Scripture can be a vital part of filling our minds with God's Word. We encourage you to give this important habit a try.

CONNECTING *with God's Family (Fellowship)*

The foundation for spiritual growth is an intimate connection with God and his family. A few people who really know you and who earn your trust provide a place to experience the life Jesus invites you to live. This section of each session typically offers you two activities. You can get to know your whole group by using the icebreaker question, and/or you can check in with one or two group members—your spiritual partner(s)—for a deeper connection and encouragement in your spiritual journey.

DVD TEACHING SEGMENT. A *Deepening Life Together: Acts* Video Teaching DVD companion to this study guide is available. For each study session, the DVD contains a lesson taught by Erik Thoennes. If you are using the DVD, you will view the teaching segment after your *Connecting* discussion and before your group discussion time (the *Growing* section). At the end of each session in this study guide, you will find space for your notes on the teaching segment.

GROWING *to Be Like Christ (Discipleship)*

Here is where you come face-to-face with Scripture. In core passages you'll explore what the Bible teaches about the topic of the study. The focus won't be on accumulating information but on how we should live in light of the Word of God. We want to help you apply the Scriptures practically, creatively, and from your heart as well as your head. At the end of the day, allowing the timeless truths from God's Word to transform our lives in Christ is our greatest aim.

DEVELOPING *Your Gifts to Serve Others (Ministry)*

Jesus trained his disciples to discover and develop their gifts to serve others. And God has designed each of us uniquely to serve him in a way no other person can. This section will help you discover and use your God-given design. It will also encourage your group to discover your unique design as a community. In this study, you'll put into practice what you've learned in the Bible study by taking a step to serve others. These simple steps will take your group on a faith journey that could change your lives forever.

SHARING *Your Life Mission Every Day (Evangelism)*

Many people skip over this aspect of the Christian life because it's scary, relationally awkward, or simply too much work for their busy schedules. But Jesus wanted all of his disciples to help outsiders connect with him, to know him personally. This doesn't mean preaching on street corners. It could mean welcoming a few newcomers into your group, hosting a short-term group in your home, or walking through this study with a friend. In this study, you'll have an opportunity to go beyond Bible study to biblical living.

SURRENDERING *Your Life for God's Pleasure (Worship)*

God is most pleased by a heart that is fully his. Each group session will give you a chance to surrender your heart to God in prayer and worship. You may read a psalm together, share a page in your journal, or sing a song to close your meeting. If you have never prayed aloud in a group before, no one will pressure you. Instead, you'll experience the support of others who are praying for you.

Study Notes

This section provides background notes on the Bible passage(s) you examine in the *Growing* section. You may want to refer to these notes during your group meeting or as a reference for those doing additional study.

For Deeper Study (Optional)

If you want to dig deeper into more Bible passages about the topic at hand, we've provided additional passages and questions. Your group may choose to do study homework ahead of each meeting in order to cover more biblical material. Or you as an individual may choose to study the *For Deeper Study* on your own. If you prefer not to do study homework, the *Growing* section will provide you with plenty to discuss within the group. These options allow individuals or the whole group to go deeper in their study, while still accommodating those who can't do homework or are new to your group.

You can record your discoveries in your journal. We encourage you to read some of your insights to a friend (spiritual partner) for accountability and support. Spiritual partners may check in each week over the phone, through e-mail, or at the beginning of the group meeting.

Reflections

On the *Reflections* pages we provide Scriptures to read and reflect on between group meetings. We suggest you use this section to seek God at home throughout the week. This time at home should begin and end with prayer. Don't get in a hurry; take enough time to hear God's direction.

Subgroup for Discussion and Prayer

If your group is large (more than seven people), we encourage you to separate into groups of two to four for discussion and prayer. This is to encourage greater participation and deeper discussion.

INTRODUCTION

Welcome to the *Deepening Life Together* Bible study on *Acts*. We will live this Bible study together during the next eight weeks as we experience God through the pages of Scripture in a mighty way, accomplishing his purpose for salvation. As we read, discuss, and reflect on the topic of each session together, our confidence in God's ability to use ordinary people to accomplish his purposes will grow to new heights. We will discover and tap into the power that fueled Jesus's commission to his disciples to take the gospel to the ends of the earth.

The next eight weeks will take us step-by-step through the stages of the gospel expansion. We will witness the explosion of the gospel message as the Spirit-filled and Spirit-empowered believers boldly proclaimed the message of salvation everywhere they went. Met by internal conflict and external persecution, the church was strengthened, forcing the gospel out of its Jerusalem confines. We'll see how the dramatic conversion of Saul set the stage for the expansion of the church to the Gentiles, a critical first step in Jesus's commission to take the gospel to all nations. In the climax and resolution to the study, we will learn that despite Paul's persecution and imprisonment the gospel is not bound as he continues to boldly proclaim God's good news, advancing it to the ends of the earth.

This journey of discovery will make known God's purposes for our lives. We will connect with our loving and faithful God and with other believers in small group community. We will become his hands and feet here on earth as he reveals our uniqueness and his willingness to use us. We will experience the closeness that he desires with us as we prayerfully respond to the principles we learn in this study and learn to place him first in our lives.

We at Baker Books and Lifetogether Publishing look forward to hearing the stories of how God changes you from the inside out during this small group experience. We pray God blesses you with all he has planned for you through this journey together.

> For the LORD is good and his love endures forever;
> his faithfulness continues through all generations.
>
> Psalm 100:5 (NIV)

BRILLIANT BEGINNINGS

Memory Verse: But you will receive power when the Holy Spirit comes on you; and you will be my witnesses in Jerusalem, and in all Judea and Samaria, and to the ends of the earth (Acts 1:8 NIV).

Every morning before school for the past year or so, John's daughter has faithfully made him a pot of coffee. He's grown accustomed to going downstairs, reaching for a mug, and simply pouring a steaming hot cup. Once in awhile, though, the carafe is empty. Only a little disappointed, John realizes that his daughter forgot to push the button to turn the coffee maker on. It's amazing how much difference power makes to a good cup of coffee.

Charles Spurgeon said, "We might preach 'til our tongue rotted, 'til we exhaust our lungs and die—but never a soul would be converted unless the Holy Spirit uses the Word to convert that soul."* Following Jesus's ascension in chapter 1 of the book of Acts, the Holy Spirit fills the apostles, empowering them to be his witnesses. The apostles might have felt confident in their ability to minister, especially having learned under the master himself, but without the power of the Holy Spirit to touch hearts, they are empty carafes.

* Peter Adam, *Speaking God's Words: A Practical Theology of Preaching* (Vancouver: Regent College Publishing, 2004).

 **Connecting**

As you begin *Session One*, ask the Lord in prayer to unify your group and challenge you as you study his Word during these next eight weeks.

Take time to pass around a copy of the *Small Group Roster* in the appendix, a sheet of paper, or one of you pass your study guide, opened to the *Small Group Roster*. Each of you write down your contact information including the best time and method for contacting you. Then, someone volunteer to make copies or type up a list with everyone's information and e-mail it to the group this week.

1. Begin this first session of *Acts* by introducing yourselves. Include your name, what you do for a living, and what you do for fun. You may also include whether or not you are married, how long you have been married, how many children you have, and their ages.

2. Whether your group is new or ongoing, it's always important to reflect on and review your values together. In the *Appendix* is a *Small Group Agreement* with the values most useful in sustaining healthy, balanced groups. Choose two or three values that you have room to grow in, or haven't previously focused on, to emphasize during this study. Doing this will take your group to the next stage of intimacy and spiritual health.

   If your group is new, you may want to focus on welcoming newcomers or on sharing group ownership. Any group will quickly move from being *the leader's group* to *our group* if everyone understands the goals of the group and shares a small role. See the *Team Roles* in the *Appendix* for help on how to do this well.

3. Share your expectations for the study. How do you hope God will challenge you?

Growing

The early days of the church described in Acts were a time of extraordinary unity, growth, and expansion, as the Spirit-filled and Spirit-empowered believers boldly proclaimed the message of salvation to the residents of Jerusalem.

4. Read Acts 1:1–11. What are the key elements of Jesus's commission to his disciples (1:8)? Why is each element important?

   What point were the two men dressed in white (v. 11) trying to get across? How does this apply to believers today?

5. Jesus instructed his disciples to stay in Jerusalem until the promised gift was given (vv. 4–5). What was the gift Jesus spoke about?

6. Read Acts 1:15–26, which tells us what the disciples did as they waited. They replaced Judas because it was symbolically important to have twelve apostles. If you know anything about the Old Testament, what did the number twelve signify?

7. Read Acts 2. What effect did the demonstration of the power of the Holy Spirit (2:1–4) have on the Jews who were present (2:5–13)?

   Verses 14–26 summarize Peter's first proclamation of the gospel. What are the central historical facts of his message (vv. 22–24, 32–33)?

   Why is the bodily resurrection of Jesus from the dead, as a historical event that really happened, central to Peter's message? According to Peter, what does the resurrection demonstrate?

8. Two gifts were given in Acts 2:37–41: forgiveness of sins and the Holy Spirit. To whom was the Spirit given and how did they receive it? (See the *Study Notes* for more information about Filled with the Spirit vs. Baptism of the Spirit.)

9. Look at the list of things to which the early church was devoted (2:42–47). Why was each of these important?

   What effect did this have on the growth in number of believers? Discuss the implication of this on the church today.

10. Peter healed a lame beggar and continued to preach in the power of the Spirit (chap. 3), despite the danger of arrest and death (chap. 4). Read Acts 4:4, and reread Acts 2:41. What do we learn about the power of the Holy Spirit through the people's responses to Peter's message?

11. What are the noteworthy elements of the believers' prayer (4:23–31) after Peter and John were arrested and eventually freed?

    What was the result of this prayer?

12. Considering question 8 and the events of Acts 2–4, how can you conclude that one becomes and remains Spirit-filled? (See the *Study Notes* for information about Filled with the Spirit vs. Baptism of the Spirit.)

13. What did Gamaliel say in Acts 5:38–39? How was it prophetic of what was to come?

14. When has the Holy Spirit enabled you to act boldly? If you can't think of a time, what might that mean?

The Holy Spirit empowered the apostles to preach the gospel boldly in spite of opposition, and thousands were added to the number of believers.

Developing

As we discovered in this session, the Holy Spirit enables believers to minister with confidence. Developing our ability to serve God according to the Holy Spirit's leading requires that we get to know God personally and intimately. We must make time for prayer, for reading God's Word, and for meditation, and invite the Holy Spirit to speak into our lives every day.

15. Which of the following steps are you willing to take for the next few weeks?

☐ **Prayer.** Commit to daily time in personal, focused prayer and connection with God. Find a place where you can be alone and undistracted. You may find it helpful to write your prayers in a journal.

☐ **Reflection.** At the end of each session, you'll find *Reflections*— Scriptures that specifically relate to the topic of our study each week. These are provided to give you an opportunity for reading a short Bible passage five days a week during the course of this study. Write down your insights on what you read each day in the space provided. On the sixth day, summarize what God has shown you throughout the week.

☐ **Meditation.** Meditation is focused attention on the Word of God—a great way to internalize God's Word more deeply. Copy a portion of Scripture on a card and tape it somewhere in your line of sight, such as your car's dashboard, the bathroom mirror, or the kitchen table. Think about it when you sit at red lights, while you get ready for your day, or while you're eating a meal. Reflect on what God is saying to you through these words. Consider using the *memory verse* and *Reflections* verses provided each week for meditation.

Sharing

Jesus commissioned all of his disciples to be his witnesses (Acts 1:8, memory verse), but he does not expect us to do it alone. As this verse tells us, we will receive power when the Holy Spirit comes on us. The Holy Spirit will enable us to confidently share Jesus with others.

16. Acts 4:13 says, "When they saw the courage of Peter and John and realized that they were unschooled, ordinary men, they were astonished and they took note that these men had been with Jesus" (NIV).

    Can anyone tell by your life that you've been with Jesus? Talk about what people see in a Christian's life that reveals Jesus.

17. During the coming week, note the people with whom you interact in your daily life. Are there people that you see casually every day, meet socially with once per week, or talk to with regularity? These are just some of the people that make up your sphere of influence or "circle of life." Next week we will take a closer look at who these people are and how Jesus might be calling you to boldly share with them.

Surrendering

Worship means to show reverent love and devotion to God. Each week you will have an opportunity to surrender your hearts to God in an attitude of worship through vocal praise and prayer.

18. Every believer should have a plan for spending time alone with God. Your time with God is individual and reflects who you are in relationship with our personal God. However you choose to spend your time with him, try to allow time for praise, prayer, and reading of Scripture. The *Reflections* provided in each session can be used in your daily time with him. These will offer reinforcement of the principles we are learning, and help you

develop or strengthen your habit of regular time alone with God.

19. Allow everyone to answer this question: "How can we pray for you this week?" Write prayer requests on your *Prayer and Praise Report* and commit to praying for each other throughout the week.

Before We Meet Again

In *Session Two*, we will be discussing Acts chapters 6 through 8. Although questions will target specific passages, it is important that you understand the context of the passages we will be studying. With this in mind, read these chapters before meeting for *Session Two*.

Study Notes

Filled with the Spirit vs. Baptism of the Spirit: Though some Christians differ in their perspective on this issue, being filled with the Spirit appears to be different from being baptized by the Spirit. The apostle Paul speaks of being baptized into Christ and receiving the Spirit as one event by which Christ places believers into his body (Rom. 6:4–6; 8:9–16; 1 Cor. 12:3, 13; Gal. 3:1–5, 26–28; 4:4–7). Nowhere in his letters does he seem to imagine a person who has put faith in Christ but who has not received the Spirit. (However, see Acts 8:15–16.)

Being filled with the Spirit, on the other hand, appears to be an ongoing experience of dependence on the Holy Spirit's power to live righteously. Although filled initially on the Day of Pentecost, Peter was filled again in Acts 4:8. Many of the same people filled with the Spirit in Acts 2 were filled again in Acts 4:31. Acts 6:5 describes Stephen as a man "full of faith and of the Holy Spirit," yet Acts 7:55 records his being filled again. Paul was filled with the Spirit in Acts 9:17 and again in Acts 13:9.

Pentecost: The fiftieth day after the Sabbath of Passover week (Lev. 23:15–16), thus the first day of the week. Pentecost is also called the Feast of Weeks (Deut. 16:10), the Feast of Harvest (Exod. 23:16), and the day of firstfruits (Num. 28:26).

Pharisees: The Pharisees were a religious party within Judaism who strictly kept the law of Moses and the unwritten "tradition of the elders." They were strong competitors and opponents of the Sadducees.

Sadducees: A Jewish sect whose members came from the priestly line and controlled the temple. They did not believe in the resurrection or a personal Messiah, but held that the messianic age—an ideal time—was then present and must be preserved. The high priest of the Sadducees presided over the Sanhedrin.

Sanhedrin: The supreme Jewish court. In New Testament times, it was made up of three kinds of members: chief priests, elders, and teachers of the law. Its total membership numbered seventy-one, including the high priest, who was presiding officer. Under Roman jurisdiction, the Sanhedrin was given a great deal of authority, but they could not impose capital punishment.

For Deeper Study (Optional)

In Acts 1:8, Jesus tells us that we will be his witnesses. In a court of law, a witness is a person who gives a testimony. The apostles had been with Jesus during his entire three years of ministry.

1. After three years with Jesus, what could they testify about him?

2. Read John 9:1–25. What was the blind man's testimony (see v. 25)? What insight does this passage give into your own testimony?

3. Read 1 John 5:6–12. Who testifies in verse 6? What is the testimony (vv. 11–12) and how do we become witnesses to it (v. 10)?

4. How does this passage bring clarity to Acts 1:8?

Reflections

Reading, reflecting, and meditating on the Word of God is essential to getting to know him deeply. As you read the verses each day, give prayerful consideration to what you learn about God, his Spirit, and his place in your life. Then record your thoughts, insights, or prayer in the *Reflect* section below the verses you read. On the sixth day, record a summary of what you learned over the entire week through this study.

Day 1. When the Counselor comes, whom I will send to you from the Father, the Spirit of truth who goes out from the Father, he will testify about me. And you also must testify, for you have been with me from the beginning (John 15:26–27 NIV).

REFLECT

_____

_____

_____

_____

Day 2. He told them, "This is what is written: The Christ will suffer and rise from the dead on the third day, and repentance and forgiveness of sins will be preached in his name to all nations, beginning at Jerusalem. You are witnesses of these things. I am going to send you what my Father has promised; but stay in the city until you have been clothed with power from on high" (Luke 24:46–49 NIV).

REFLECT

Day 3. I baptize you with water for repentance. But after me will come one who is more powerful than I, whose sandals I am not fit to carry. He will baptize you with the Holy Spirit and with fire (Matt. 3:11 NIV).

REFLECT

Day 4. Create in me a pure heart, O God, and renew a steadfast spirit within me. Do not cast me from your presence or take your Holy Spirit from me. Restore to me the joy of your salvation and grant me a willing spirit, to sustain me (Ps. 51:10–12 NIV).

REFLECT

Day 5. All the believers were one in heart and mind. No one claimed that any of his possessions was his own, but they shared everything they had. With great power the apostles continued to testify to the resurrection of the Lord Jesus, and much grace was upon them all. There were no needy persons among them. For from time to time those who owned lands or houses sold them, brought the money from the sales and put it at the apostles' feet, and it was distributed to anyone as he had need (Acts 4:32–35 NIV).

REFLECT

_____

_____

_____

_____

Day 6. Use the following space to write any thoughts God has put in your heart and mind about the things we have looked at in this session and during your *Reflections* time this week.

SUMMARY

_____

_____

_____

_____

OPPOSITION AND EXPANSION

Memory Verse: Those who had been scattered preached the word wherever they went (Acts 8:4 NIV).

In an unconfirmed story, a famous Chinese Christian, Watchman Nee, was scheduled to speak at a gathering where he knew government spies would be present. Wanting to avoid certain arrest, but not wanting to disappoint those gathered, he picked up a glass of water that was near him and threw it to the floor, smashing it with his heel repeatedly in mock arrogance. The more he stomped on the glass, the farther the glass spread.

The spies didn't know what was happening, but the believers understood his unspoken message clearly. As Nee represented the government, and the glass represented the church, he was demonstrating that in an attempt to destroy the church, the enemy had served as God's instrument in its growth.

Matthew Henry wrote in his *Commentary on the Whole Bible*, "The enemies designed to scatter and lose them, Christ designed to scatter and use them." As the first century believers grew in number, so did the Jews' determination to stomp out the church, but God used their vain attempts to strengthen and spread it.

Connecting

Begin your group time with prayer. Ask God to challenge you in a new way through today's session.

1. If you have new people joining you for the first time, take a few minutes to briefly introduce yourselves. Then, share one thing God revealed to you last week about the power of the Holy Spirit.

2. Healthy small groups rotate leadership. We recommend that you rotate leaders on a regular basis. This practice helps to develop every member's ability to shepherd a few people within a safe environment. Even Jesus gave others the opportunity to serve alongside him (Mark 6:30–44).

   It's also a good idea to rotate host homes, with the host of each meeting providing the refreshments. Some groups like to let the host lead the meeting each week, while others like to allow one person to host while another person leads.

   The *Small Group Calendar* in the *Appendix* is a tool for planning who will lead and host each meeting. Take a few minutes to plan leaders and hosts for your remaining meetings. Don't pass up this opportunity! It will revolutionize your group.

   For information on leading your group, see the *Leader's Notes (Introduction)* and notes for the session you will be leading in the *Appendix*. Also, if you are leading for the first time, see *Leading for the First Time (Leadership 101)* in the *Appendix*. If you still have questions about rotating hosts and/or homes, refer to the *Frequently Asked Questions (FAQs)* in the *Appendix*.

3. Can you think of a time in your life when a bad experience turned into a blessing for you or someone you know? A few of you share your experiences and outcomes.

 **Growing**

As the Holy Spirit empowers the apostles to preach the gospel boldly, the church experiences rapid growth. In Acts 6–8, believers encounter internal conflict as well as external persecution.

4. A problem is brought to the apostles' attention in Acts 6:1–7. What is the problem, and how is it resolved?

    How does the resolution of the problem demonstrate unity and further spread the gospel message?

5. Acts 6:8–7:53 describes the ministry of Stephen, a man full of God's grace and power, and the opposition he faces that leads to his martyrdom. What does Stephen say to his oppressors in 7:51–53?

6. Read Acts 7:54–60. How does the Sanhedrin respond to Stephen's message?

    What words does Stephen speak in 7:59–60? Compare these words to those Jesus spoke in Luke 23:34, 46. What is the significance of Stephen's words?

7. Read Acts 8:1–4. What effect does the stoning of Stephen have on the church? What do the scattered believers do?

8. How do you see the Holy Spirit at work in Philip's ministry (8:5–13, 26–40)?

9. Have you ever experienced a prompting of the Holy Spirit to act? If so, share what you did and what resulted.

Although persecution of the early church was intended to stop God's movement, his unstoppable plan advanced in an explosion of evangelism throughout the region.

Developing

God has designed each of us uniquely with individual talents, abilities, passions, and experiences that determine where we serve within the body of Christ. In order to begin this journey of discovering how God made us, it's important to be sure that we live consistently and honestly. One way that we can ensure that the way we live our lives agrees with the faith we profess is through spiritual accountability.

10. We strongly recommend each of you partner with someone in the group to help you in your spiritual journey during this study. This person will be your spiritual partner for the next several weeks. Pair up with someone in your group now (men partner with men and women with women) and turn to the *Personal Health Plan* in the *Appendix*.

    In the box that says, "WHO are you connecting with spiritually?" write your partner's name. In the box that says, "WHAT is your next step for growth?" write one step you would like to take for growth during this study. Tell your partner what step you chose. When you check in with your partner each week, the "Partner's Progress" column on this chart will provide a place to record your partner's progress in the goal he or she chose.

11. Spending time getting to know each other outside of group meetings is helpful to building stronger relationships within your group. Discuss whether your group would like to have a potluck or other type of social to celebrate together what God is doing in your group. You could plan to share a meal prior to a small group meeting or plan to follow your completion of this study with a barbecue. Appoint one or two people who can follow up with everyone outside of group time to put a plan together.

Sharing

Jesus's commission in Acts 1:8 included witnessing in Jerusalem, Judea, and Samaria, and to the ends of the earth. This is a model for us in identifying our starting point for sharing Jesus with others. Your Jerusalem is the city in which you live and includes your family, friends, neighbors, coworkers, etc.

12. Take a look at the *Circles of Life* diagram below and think of people you know in each category who need to be connected in Christian community. Write the names of two or three people in each circle.

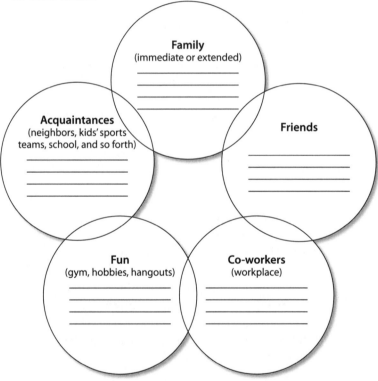

The people who fill these circles are not there by accident. God has strategically placed each of them within your sphere of influence because he has equipped you to minister to them and share with them in ways no one else can. Consider the following ideas for reaching out to one or two of the people you listed and make a plan to follow through with them this week.

☐ This is a wonderful time to welcome a few friends into your group. Which of the people you listed could you invite? It's possible that you may need to help your friend overcome obstacles to coming to a place where he or she can encounter Jesus. Does your friend need a ride to the group or help with child care?

☐ Consider inviting a friend to attend a weekend church service with you and possibly plan to enjoy a meal together afterward. This can be a great opportunity to talk with someone about your faith in Jesus.

☐ Is there someone who is unable to attend your group but who still needs a connection? Would you be willing to have lunch or coffee with that person, catch up on life, and share something you've learned from this study? Jesus doesn't call all of us to lead small groups, but he does call every disciple to spiritually multiply his or her life over time.

Surrendering

Paul tells us in Romans 6:13, "Do not offer the parts of your body to sin, as instruments of wickedness, but rather offer yourselves to God, as those who have been brought from death to life; and offer the parts of your body to him as instruments of righteousness" (NIV). One of the most difficult parts of our body to surrender to God is our mouth, yet God tells us to offer it as an instrument of righteousness. Difficult as it may be, it is possible with the Lord's help.

13. Romans 12:14 tells us, "Bless those who persecute you; bless and do not curse" (NIV). In question 4, you were asked when you have been blessed through a bad situation in your life. Maybe you're currently in a situation where you feel you are being mistreated, misunderstood, or are just in general conflict

with someone. Surrender that situation to the Lord in prayer right now. Ask him to help you see his plan in your situation and for strength to endure.

14. Think about what it would take for you to make time with God a priority every day or even five or six days a week. What obstacles prevent you from following through? You don't need to demand an hour or even a half hour of time at first; consider drawing near to God for a few minutes each day and gradually you will desire more. Don't forget, you can use the Reflections at the end of each session as a starting point for drawing near to God.

15. Share your prayer requests in your group and then gather in smaller circles of three or four people to pray. Be sure to have everyone write down the personal requests of the members to use as a reminder to pray throughout the week.

    Then pray for one another in your circle. Don't put pressure on anyone to pray aloud. When you pray for each person, you may find it meaningful to hold hands or place your hands on another person's shoulder. Jesus often touched those he healed to communicate his care for them.

Study Notes

Greek-speaking (Hellenistic) Jews: Jews born outside Palestine who spoke Greek as their primary language.

Hebraic Jews: Native Palestinian Jews who spoke Aramaic as their primary language.

Laid Their Hands on Them: In the New Testament, laying on of hands is done to heal (Acts 28:8; Mark 1:41), bless (Mark 10:16), ordain or commission (Acts 6:6; 13:3; 1 Tim. 5:22), and impart spiritual gifts (Acts 8:17; 19:6; 1 Tim. 4:14; 2 Tim. 1:6).

For Deeper Study (Optional)

1. What does Matthew 5:10–11 tell us about persecution?

2. What insight do the following passages give us about why persecution or trials might be allowed in our lives?

   ☐ Romans 5:3–5

   ☐ James 1:2–4

   ☐ 1 Peter 1:6–9

3. Read the parable of the sower in Mark 4:3–20. What does this parable teach us about what is necessary to endure persecution?

Reflections

Hopefully last week you made a commitment to read, reflect, and meditate on the Word of God each day. Following are selections of Scripture provided as a starting point to drawing near to God through time with him. Read the daily verses and then record your thoughts, insights, or prayers in the space provided. On the sixth day, record a summary of what you have learned over the entire week through this study or use this space to write down how God has challenged you personally.

Day 1. Who shall separate us from the love of Christ? Shall trouble or hardship or persecution or famine or nakedness or danger or sword? As it is written: "For your sake we face death all day long; we are considered as sheep to be slaughtered." No, in all these things we are more than conquerors through him who loved us (Rom. 8:35–37 NIV).

REFLECT

_____

_____

_____

_____

31

Day 2. So the word of God spread. The number of disciples in Jerusalem increased rapidly, and a large number of priests became obedient to the faith (Acts 6:7 NIV).

REFLECT

_____

_____

_____

_____

Day 3. Opposition arose, however, from members of the Synagogue of the Freedmen (as it was called)—Jews of Cyrene and Alexandria as well as the provinces of Cilicia and Asia. These men began to argue with Stephen, but they could not stand up against his wisdom or the Spirit by whom he spoke (Acts 6:9–10 NIV).

REFLECT

_____

_____

_____

_____

Day 4. We had previously suffered and been insulted in Philippi, as you know, but with the help of our God we dared to tell you his gospel in spite of strong opposition (1 Thess. 2:2 NIV).

REFLECT

_____

_____

_____

_____

Day 5. Those who had been scattered preached the word wherever they went (Acts 8:4 NIV).

REFLECT

_____

_____

_____

_____

Day 6. Use this space to record insights, thoughts, or prayers that God has given you during *Session Two* and your *Reflections* time.

SUMMARY

_____

_____

_____

_____

A PERSECUTOR TURNS APOSTLE

Memory Verse: But for that very reason I was shown mercy so that in me, the worst of sinners, Christ Jesus might display his unlimited patience as an example for those who would believe on him and receive eternal life (1 Tim. 1:16 NIV).

A couple of years ago, Jacob's parents retired and sold their home in sunny Southern California to travel the "open road." Even though their fifth-wheel RV was loaded with tons of amenities, they left behind many of the comforts of their home like a spacious shower, dishwasher, and the ability to get running water or electricity without first hooking up. They were beginning a new phase of life that would require a totally different lifestyle than the one they previously lived.

Second Corinthians 5:17 says, "Therefore, if anyone is in Christ, he is a new creation; the old has gone, the new has come!" (NIV). In the ninth chapter of Acts, Saul underwent remarkable life transformation. He not only left the comforts of home to preach the gospel, but he left his religious and business associates, his heritage, and his way of life—everything that had once formed who he was. All that he considered important he now considered them rubbish so that he might begin a new life and gain the surpassing greatness of knowing Christ Jesus (Phil. 3:8).

Connecting

As you open in prayer, ask the Holy Spirit to reveal specific action steps for each individual during this session.

1. Most people want to live a healthy, balanced life. A regular medical checkup is a good way to measure health and spot potential problems. In the same way, a spiritual checkup is vital to your spiritual well-being. The *Personal Health Assessment* was designed to give you a quick snapshot, or pulse, of your spiritual health.

   Take a few minutes alone to complete the *Personal Health Assessment*, found in the *Appendix*. After answering each question, tally your results. Then, pair up with your spiritual partner, and briefly share one purpose that is going well and one that needs a little work. Then go to the *Personal Health Plan* in the *Appendix* and record one next step you plan to take in the area of the purpose you want to work on. If you haven't established your spiritual partnership yet, do it now. (Refer to the *Leader's Notes Developing* section in the *Appendix* for help.)

2. What is one thing about you—your character or the way you live—that is different (from the way you otherwise would be) because of Christ?

Growing

In *Session Two* we saw the beginning of persecution against followers of Christ. One of the leading persecutors was Saul, a Pharisee. A zealous Jew who kept the law scrupulously, Saul was outraged that a man crucified as a criminal could be proclaimed as Messiah, and he was outrageous in his tactics to stamp out this new group.

3. According to 7:57–8:1, what role did Saul play in Stephen's death? What do you think it meant that the witnesses laid their clothes at Saul's feet?

4. From 7:57–8:3 and 26:9–11, how was Saul involved in the persecution?

5. What was Saul's reason for traveling to Damascus, according to 9:1–2?

   What happened to him along the way?

   Read Acts 9:1–31 aloud, taking turns around the group.

6. Why do you think Jesus revealed himself to Saul in such a dramatic way?

7. Why was Ananias afraid to visit Saul (9:13–14)?

   How did the Lord allay his fears (9:15–16)?

   What happened as a result of Ananias's visit?

8. There's a symbolic element to Saul's three days of blindness. What might that experience have taught Saul?

9. Saul changed 180 degrees and began preaching for Jesus as zealously as he had preached against him. What impressions of Saul do you get from the ways various people responded to him (9:20–25)?

10. When Saul went to Jerusalem, the disciples were afraid of him. What reasons did they have to be skeptical of his conversion?

11. Some Jews conspired against Saul (9:23, 29). Why do you think they targeted him while they left the other disciples alone?

12. After Saul left Jerusalem for Tarsus, the church experienced a time of peace. Discuss how these events might be related.

13. Contrast 9:1 and 9:29. Has the Holy Spirit ever prompted a drastic transformation of your thinking? If so, what changed? How did others respond to the change in you?

Saul's sudden and dramatic conversion resulted in a miraculous transformation as he went from outrageous persecutor of the church, responsible for punishing, imprisoning, and executing disciples, to God's chosen instrument to carry the name of Christ to the Gentiles. Not all conversions are so dramatic. (Peter, for example, had a number of milestones on the way to Acts 2, not just one.) But Saul (also known by his Roman name, Paul) is the most famous example of a sudden turnabout.

Developing

God created each of us to serve him within the body of Christ. According to 1 Peter 4:10, which says, "As each one has received a gift, minister it to one another, as good stewards of the manifold grace of God" (NKJV), every believer has been given at least one spiritual gift for the purpose of filling specific needs within the body of Christ—the church.

14. Discuss some ways that we can serve the body of Christ. If you are already serving somewhere, share your experiences with the group.

   If you are not currently serving, is there a particular area of service that God has put on your heart to serve either this group or your local church? If not, pray about finding a ministry in which you can serve. As you take that first step, God will lead you to the ministry that expresses your passion.

Sharing

All around you, people are searching for purpose. As you live out God's purpose for your life, you become a visible reminder of God's design for others.

15. Matthew 5:16 says, "Let your light shine before men, that they may see your good deeds and praise your Father in heaven" (NIV). In the last session you wrote some names in the *Circles of Life* diagram. Have you followed up with those you identified who need to connect with other Christians? If not, when will you contact them?

    Go back to the *Circles of Life* diagram to remind yourself of the names you wrote there. Then commit to following through. Share your commitment with your spiritual partner and pray together for God to help you let his light shine through you.

16. Today we learned about Saul's dramatic encounter with Jesus on the road to Damascus and his subsequent conversion. Jesus desires to enter each of our lives in a dramatic and life-changing way. If Saul's story has encouraged you and you have never invited Jesus to take control of your life, why not ask him now? If you are not clear about God's gift of eternal life for everyone who believes in Jesus and how to receive this gift, take a minute to pray and ask God to help you understand what he wants you to do about trusting in Jesus.

Surrendering

Prayer is one of the ways that we enter into the presence of God. James 5:16 says, "Therefore confess your sins to each other and pray for each other so that you may be healed. The prayer of a righteous man is powerful and effective" (NIV). As we confess our sins and burdens to one another and commit to pray for one another, we will begin to experience the power of God to change lives.

17. Spend a few minutes right now sharing your praises and prayer requests. Record these on the *Prayer and Praise Report*. Then, pair up with someone and spend time now praying for each other.

18. The *Deepening Life Together: Acts* Video Teaching DVD companion for this study includes worship songs for use during your study. Choose one of these to end your study today. If you don't have the teaching DVD, use a worship CD, sing together a cappella, or ask someone who plays a musical instrument to lead the group in song.

Study Notes

Damascus. The city of Damascus, the capital of Syria, had a large population of Jews and served as a commercial hub for trade caravans. If Christianity took root and flourished in the city of Damascus, it would quickly spread into the surrounding regions. It is for this reason that Saul was determined to persecute the Christians there.

For Deeper Study (Optional)

1. List Paul's accomplishments found in Acts 26:9–11 and Galatians 1:13–14.

2. Read Paul's testimony found in Philippians 3:4–14. To what did Paul credit his righteousness in verses 4–6?

3. How did that change in verses 7–11?

4. To what does Paul commit his life in verses 12–14?

5. Read 2 Corinthians 11:16–29. How does this list of accomplishments compare to the list you compiled above?

6. Second Corinthians 5:17 says, "This means that anyone who belongs to Christ has become a new person. The old life is gone; a new life has begun!" (NLT). How does Paul's life exemplify this verse?

Reflections

If you've been spending time each day connecting with God through his Word, congratulations! Some experts say that it takes twenty-one repetitions to develop a new habit. By the end of this week, you'll be well on your way to cultivating new spiritual habits that will encourage you in your walk with God. This week, continue to read the daily verses, giving prayerful consideration to what you learn about God, his Spirit, and his place in your life. Then, as before, record your thoughts, insights, or prayers in the space provided. On the sixth day, record a summary of what you have learned throughout the week.

Day 1. I thank Christ Jesus our Lord, who has given me strength, that he considered me faithful, appointing me to his service. Even though I was once a blasphemer and a persecutor and a violent man, I was shown mercy because I acted in ignorance and unbelief. The grace of our Lord was poured out on me abundantly, along with the faith and love that are in Christ Jesus (1 Tim. 1:12–14 NIV).

REFLECT

_____

_____

_____

_____

Day 2. For I am the least of the apostles and do not even deserve to be called an apostle, because I persecuted the church of God. But by the grace of God I am what I am (1 Cor. 15:9–10 NIV).

REFLECT

_____

_____

_____

_____

Day 3. But the Lord said to Ananias, "Go! This man is my chosen instrument to carry my name before the Gentiles and their kings and before the people of Israel. I will show him how much he must suffer for my name" (Acts 9:15–16 NIV).

REFLECT

_____

_____

_____

_____

Day 4. I will also make you a light for the Gentiles, that you may bring my salvation to the ends of the earth (Isa. 49:6 NIV).

REFLECT

_____

_____

_____

_____

Day 5. I have become its servant by the commission God gave me to present to you the word of God in its fullness—the mystery that has been kept hidden for ages and generations, but is now disclosed to the saints. To them God has chosen to make known among the

Gentiles the glorious riches of this mystery, which is Christ in you, the hope of glory (Col. 1:25–27 NIV).

REFLECT

_____

_____

_____

_____

Day 6. Record your weekly summary of what God has shown you in the space below.

SUMMARY

_____

_____

_____

_____

INTO ALL THE WORLD

Memory Verse: Then Peter began to speak: "I now realize how true it is that God does not show favoritism but accepts men from every nation who fear him and do what is right" (Acts 10:34–35 NIV).

As William Booth preached salvation to the thieves, prostitutes, gamblers, and drunkards of the London slums in 1865, his aim was to convert them and then connect them to a local church where they could be discipled. But, the Church of England was hostile toward his endeavors and refused to accept the converts because of what they had been. This ill will drove him to found what is now called the Salvation Army. He says of his own motivation, "I saw multitudes of my fellow-creatures not only without God and hope, but sunk in the most desperate forms of wickedness and misery that can be conceived."*

Since that time, the Salvation Army has expanded into 111 countries and continues to serve the poor and needy in the areas of addiction dependency, health services, social work, and emergency services. Its mission is simple: to preach the gospel of Jesus Christ and to meet human needs in his name without discrimination.

Acts 10:34–35 tells us that God does not show favoritism. He doesn't care about an individual's station in life, nationality, or material possessions, but accepts everyone who calls on his name.

* Harold Begbie, *The Life of General William Booth, the Founder of the Salvation Army* (New York: Macmillan, 1920).

Connecting

Open your group with prayer. Thank God for how he's challenged you during the previous weeks of this study of Acts. Ask him to open your hearts and impact each person with the message this week.

1. Check in with your spiritual partner, or with another partner if yours is absent. Turn to your *Personal Health Plan*. Share with your partner how your time with God went this week. What is one thing you discovered? Or, what hindered you from following through? Make a note about your partner's progress and how you can pray for him or her.

2. Have you ever felt like an outsider excluded from the in group? If so, what was that like for you?

Growing

God's divine appointment for Cornelius and Peter sets the stage for gospel expansion to the Gentiles.
Read Acts 10:1–48.

3. What impression do you get of Cornelius from 10:1–2?

4. The Lord gave Cornelius a vision (10:3–8). What did the vision instruct him to do? How did he respond?

5. Read the *Study Notes* and then explain what you think was the meaning of the vision Peter received in 10:9–23. How did it prepare him for his visit with Cornelius?

6. How did Peter's realization in Acts 10:34–35 set the stage for evangelism to all people?

7. In Acts 9, the Lord told Ananias that Saul was his chosen instrument to take the gospel to the Gentiles. Considering this, why do you think God had Peter share Christ with a Gentile family before Saul got started?

44

Read Acts 11:1–18.

8. Cornelius and his household were baptized into the body of believers as a result of Peter's visit. How did Jewish believers react to the news of Peter sharing the Word of God with Gentiles (11:1–3)?

9. In verses 15–17, what did Peter say to quell the objections of Jewish Christians?

How did they respond? Why was this acceptance by Jewish Christians pivotal to the spread of the gospel?

10. If not for the leading of the Holy Spirit, Peter might have allowed his prejudice to keep him from preaching to the Gentiles. Have you ever refrained from sharing Jesus with someone because of a social bias? If so, when? If not, what other things sometimes hinder you from sharing the gospel?

Peter's willingness to meet with Cornelius and share the gospel with him and his household bridged the gap between Jew and Gentile and served as a critical first step in Jesus's commission to take the gospel to all nations.

Developing

Last week we talked about serving God in the body of Christ. First Peter 4:10 says, "Each one should use whatever gift he has received to serve others, faithfully administering God's grace in its various forms" (NIV). If we are to effectively administer God's grace to others, we must discover and develop the gifts that God has given us.

11. The Bible reveals the many spiritual gifts given to believers. Take five minutes and review the *Spiritual Gifts Inventory* in the *Appendix*. Discuss which of the listed gifts you believe you may have.

Once you have an idea about what your spiritual gifts are, discuss how your specific gift(s) might meet a need within your small group. For example, the gift of administration might meet the need to keep the roster updated; or the gift of hospitality might be used to plan a group social activity.

Sharing

Matthew 25:37–40 says, "'Lord, when did we see you hungry and feed you, or thirsty and give you something to drink? When did we see you a stranger and invite you in, or needing clothes and clothe you? When did we see you sick or in prison and go to visit you?' The King will reply, 'I tell you the truth, whatever you did for one of the least of these brothers of mine, you did for me'" (NIV). As Jesus preached to his disciples in this passage, he taught that as we show love for others, we are showing love for him. We can share the love of Jesus with others through our actions.

12. In *Session Two*, you identified people within your *Circles of Life* who needed connection to Christian community. Jesus's commission in Acts 1:8 included sharing him not only within our own circles of influence (our Jerusalem), but also in Judea and Samaria and the ends of the earth. Judea included the region in which Jerusalem was located. Today, this might include neighboring communities or cities. As a group, discuss the following possible actions you can take to share Jesus with your Judea in a tangible way. Here are a few ideas:

   ☐ Collect new blankets and/or socks for the homeless. Bring them with you next week and have someone deliver them to a ministry serving the homeless in a nearby city.

   ☐ Bring nonperishable food items to group next week and designate one person to donate them to a local food bank.

   ☐ As a group, pick a night to volunteer to serve meals at a downtown mission or homeless shelter.

13. Telling your own story is a powerful way to share Jesus with others. Turn to *Telling Your Story* in the *Appendix*. Review this with your Spiritual Partner. Begin developing your story by taking a few minutes to share briefly what your life was like before you knew Christ. (If you haven't yet committed your life to Christ or are not sure, you can find information about this in the Sharing section of *Session Three*. If you became a Christian at a very young age and don't remember what life was like before Christ, reflect on what you have seen in the life of someone close to you.) Make notes about this aspect of your story below and commit to writing it out this week. Then, spend some time individually developing your complete story using the *Telling Your Story* exercise in the *Appendix*.

Surrendering

First John 3:11 says, "This is the message you heard from the beginning: We should love one another" (NIV). One way to show your love for one another is to pray focused prayer over each other's needs.

14. Take some time now to begin the Circle of Prayer exercise. This exercise allows for focused prayer over each person or couple in the group. Each person or couple will have an opportunity to share any pressing needs, concerns, or struggles requiring prayer, and the rest of the group will pray for these requests. More complete instructions for this can be found in the *Leader's Notes*.

15. Have one person close this session in prayer, making sure to thank God for all he's done in and through your group to this point.

Study Notes

Four-footed Animals: God set specific dietary restrictions regarding the consumption of certain animals in order to separate the Israelites from their idolatrous neighbors (Leviticus 11). Both clean and unclean animals were represented on the sheet.

Kill and Eat: Under the new covenant established by Jesus Christ, God ended the dietary restrictions. Not only was God abolishing the dietary restrictions, he was uniting the Jews, symbolized by the clean animals, with the Gentiles, symbolized by the unclean animals.

Gentile: All non-Jewish people.

For Deeper Study (Optional)

During this week's session, we learned that God revealed to Peter that the Gentiles were ready to receive the gospel. Read Romans 11:11–24.

1. Paul is teaching that since the Jews rejected the gospel, he has made it available to the Gentiles. What question does he ask in verse 11 and how does he answer it?

2. Paul tells us that some of the branches from Abraham's tree have been broken off and branches from the wild olive tree have been grafted in. What is the significance of being grafted into Abraham's tree?

3. What is Paul's warning in verses 18–24? Why does he offer this warning?

4. What does this passage teach about God's mercy to both the Jews and the Gentiles?

Reflections

Second Timothy 3:16–17 reads, "All Scripture is God-breathed and is useful for teaching, rebuking, correcting and training in righteousness, so that the man of God may be thoroughly equipped for every good work . . ." (NIV). Allow God's Word to train you in righteousness as you read, reflect on, and respond to the Scripture in your daily time with God this week.

Day 1. Then Paul and Barnabas answered them boldly: "We had to speak the word of God to you first. Since you reject it and do not consider yourselves worthy of eternal life, we now turn to the Gentiles" (Acts 13:46 NIV).

REFLECT

_____

_____

_____

_____

Day 2. Therefore I want you to know that God's salvation has been sent to the Gentiles, and they will listen! (Acts 28:28 NIV)

REFLECT

_____

_____

_____

_____

Day 3. The Lord is not slow in keeping his promise, as some understand slowness. He is patient with you, not wanting anyone to perish, but everyone to come to repentance (2 Peter 3:9 NIV).

REFLECT

_____

_____

_____

_____

Day 4. The Scriptures foresaw that God would justify the Gentiles by faith, and announced the gospel in advance to Abraham: "All nations will be blessed through you." So those who have faith are blessed along with Abraham, the man of faith (Gal. 3:8–9 NIV).

REFLECT

_____

_____

_____

_____

Day 5. For we are God's workmanship, created in Christ Jesus to do good works, which God prepared in advance for us to do (Eph. 2:10 NIV).

REFLECT

_____

_____

_____

_____

Day 6. Use the following space to record your summary of how God has challenged you this week.

SUMMARY

_____

_____

_____

_____

PETER'S DELIVERANCE

Memory Verse: But the word of God continued to increase and spread (Acts 12:24 NIV).

John G. Paton was a Scottish missionary in the island of Tanna in New Hebrides in the 1800s. In those days, the hostile natives were thought to be cannibals. One night the natives surrounded the mission headquarters where Paton and his wife were staying intending to kill them. Paton and his wife prayed all night long for God's protection and in the morning saw their attackers had gone.

Years later, after the chief had become a Christian, when asked why they had not attacked that night, the chief said it was because of the hundreds of men in shining garments with drawn swords surrounding the mission.

Paul tells us in 2 Corinthians 1:10–11a, "He has delivered us from such a deadly peril, and he will deliver us. On him we have set our hope that he will continue to deliver us, as you help us by your prayers" (NIV). In Acts 12, we will read another story of miraculous deliverance by God's angels as a result of the believers' earnest prayers.

Connecting

Begin your time together in prayer. Pray according to Psalm 19:14, which says, "May the words of my mouth and the meditation of my heart be pleasing in your sight, O LORD, my Rock and my Redeemer" (NIV).

1. Check in with your spiritual partner, or with another partner if yours is absent. Talk about any challenges you are currently facing in reaching the goals you have set throughout this study. Tell your spiritual partner how he or she has encouraged you with each step. Be sure to write down your partner's progress.

2. Share one thing from last week's session that has made a lasting impression or was particularly challenging to you.

Growing

The church faced another crisis when Herod Agrippa I (the grandson of Herod the Great) executed James and arrested Peter.
    Read Acts 12.

3. James, one of Jesus's closest disciples, was the first apostle to be martyred (12:2). What potential effects, either positive or negative, do you think this incident might have had on the early church?

4. What do you think the level of security assigned to guard Peter (12:4) says about the government's view of this prisoner?

    What do you make of the fact that God allowed James to be executed but rescued Peter in an extraordinary demonstration of power?

5. The believers were praying earnestly to God for Peter while he was imprisoned (12:5). What does this teach us about how we, as believers, should handle times of crisis in the church?

6. Look at how Peter was received at Mary's house after his deliverance (12:14–17). Why do you think God's answer to their prayer astonished the believers?

What effect do you think this had on their faith?

7. Why do you think Herod responded as he did to the discovery of Peter's escape (Acts 12:18–19)?

8. Look at Acts 12:21–23. What is the irony in Herod's acceptance of acclaim (v. 22) and God's judgment (v. 23)?

By putting this account of Herod's death right after the account of what Herod did to James and Peter, the author of Acts (Luke) implies a connection between these events. What connection do you think Luke means us to see?

9. How does Acts 12 further demonstrate that God's plan is unstoppable?

How does this encourage you in your walk with Christ today?

Although the church suffers persecution and oppression, God works in mighty ways. Peter was miraculously delivered from his chains, Herod Agrippa paid the price for his arrogance, and God's unstoppable gospel advanced.

Developing

During previous sessions, we've discussed how God has given every believer spiritual gifts to serve him within the body of Christ and how to translate those gifts into ministry to our small group.

10. This week, discuss how you may be able to use your gifts to serve beyond this small group to the ministries in your church. Plan to investigate the opportunities available to you and get

involved in serving the body of Christ. It's amazing to experience God using you to fill a specific need within his church.

11. On your *Personal Health Plan*, next to the "Develop" icon, answer the "WHERE are you serving?" question. If you are not currently serving, note one area where you will consider serving and commit to praying for the right opportunity and time to begin.

12. During *Session Two*, you should have discussed whether your group would like to have a potluck or social. Take a few minutes now to tie up any loose ends in your plan.

Sharing

Saint Francis of Assisi has been quoted as saying: "Preach the Gospel always, and if necessary, use words." A godly example can be an effective witness to others of the power of Jesus to change lives.

13. In previous sessions you were asked identify people who need to be connected in Christian community. Return to the *Circles of Life* diagram. In each circle, write down one or two names of people you know who need to know Christ. Commit first to living as a godly example to those around you. Then pray for an opportunity to share Jesus with each of them. You may invite them to attend an outreach event with you or you may feel led to share the good news with him or her over coffee. Share your commitment with your spiritual partner. Pray together for God's Holy Spirit to give you the words to speak with boldness.

Surrendering

Philippians 4:6 tells us, "Do not be anxious about anything, but in everything, by prayer and petition, with thanksgiving, present your requests to God" (NIV). Prayer represents a powerful act of surrender to the Lord as we put aside our pride and lay our burdens at his feet.

14. Last week you began praying for the specific needs of each person or couple in the group during the Circle of Prayer exercise. Take some time now to pray over those for whom the group hasn't yet prayed. As you did last week, allow each individual or couple to share whatever specific needs or challenges they are facing. Then have that person or couple stand, sit, or kneel in the middle of the room. Join hands around them, or place your hands on their shoulders if everyone is comfortable doing that, and take turns praying for the specific needs shared. Ask for God's transforming power to bring change to the situations at hand.

Study Notes

Herod: Herod Agrippa I was the grandson of Herod the Great. He eventually became ruler over much of Palestine, including Judea and Samaria. He sought favor with the Jews by his persecution of Christians.

Caesarea: This coastal city served as Roman administrative headquarters for Judea. While Judea was ruled by procurators (Roman governors appointed by the emperor) during most of the first century, during this brief period (AD 41–44) the Jewish king Agrippa I ruled Judea.

For Deeper Study (Optional)

Read the following verses and write down what you learn about how God delivers his people.

1. Call upon me in the day of trouble; I will deliver you, and you will honor me (Psalm 50:15 NIV).

2. For he will deliver the needy who cry out, the afflicted who have no one to help (Psalm 72:12 NIV).

3. Do not say, "I'll pay you back for this wrong!" Wait for the LORD, and he will deliver you (Proverbs 20:22 NIV).

4. Indeed, in our hearts we felt the sentence of death. But this happened that we might not rely on ourselves but on God, who raises the dead. He has delivered us from such a deadly peril, and he will deliver us. On him we have set our hope that he will continue to deliver us, as you help us by your prayers (2 Corinthians 1:9–11a NIV).

5. And lead us not into temptation, but deliver us from the evil one (Matthew 6:13 NIV).

Reflections

The Lord promised Joshua success and prosperity in Joshua 1:8 when he said, "Do not let this Book of the Law depart from your mouth; meditate on it day and night, so that you may be careful to do everything written in it. Then you will be prosperous and successful" (NIV). We too can claim this promise for our lives as we commit to meditate on the Word of God each day. As in previous weeks, read and meditate on the daily verses and record any prayers or insights you gain in the space provided. Summarize what you have learned this week on Day 6.

Day 1. But how is it to your credit if you receive a beating for doing wrong and endure it? But if you suffer for doing good and you endure it, this is commendable before God (1 Peter 2:20 NIV).

REFLECT

_____

_____

_____

_____

Day 2. He has delivered us from such a deadly peril, and he will deliver us. On him we have set our hope that he will continue to deliver us, as you help us by your prayers. Then many will give thanks on our behalf for the gracious favor granted us in answer to the prayers of many (2 Cor. 1:10–11 NIV).

REFLECT

_____

_____

_____

_____

Day 3. Help me, O LORD my God; save me in accordance with your love. Let them know that it is your hand, that you, O LORD, have done it (Ps. 109:26–27 NIV).

REFLECT

_____

_____

_____

_____

Day 4. But even if you should suffer for what is right, you are blessed. "Do not fear what they fear; do not be frightened." But in your hearts set apart Christ as Lord. Always be prepared to give an answer to everyone who asks you to give the reason for the hope that you have. But do this with gentleness and respect, keeping a clear conscience, so that those who speak maliciously against your good behavior in Christ may be ashamed of their slander (1 Peter 3:14–16 NIV).

REFLECT

_____

_____

_____

_____

Day 5. Dear friends, do not be surprised at the painful trial you are suffering, as though something strange were happening to you. But rejoice that you participate in the sufferings of Christ, so that you may be overjoyed when his glory is revealed (1 Peter 4:12–13 NIV).

REFLECT

_____

_____

_____

_____

Day 6. Use the following space to write any thoughts God has put in your heart and mind during *Session Five* and your *Reflections* time this week.

SUMMARY

_____

_____

_____

_____

TRADITION CHALLENGES INNOVATION
THE JERUSALEM COUNCIL

Memory Verse: We believe it is through the grace of our Lord Jesus that we are saved, just as they are (Acts 15:11 NIV).

The Broadway musical, *Fiddler on the Roof,* is a classic tale of one man's struggle to hold on to family and religions traditions against the pressures of innovation. The story centers on Tevye, a milkman, who wrestles to maintain balance in his life by hanging on to time-honored customs, even though he doesn't know where they began. In rebellion against their father's ideals, his daughters refuse to accept husbands chosen for them by the matchmaker and choose instead to marry men they love. Tevye eventually must accept the changing times and adjust his way of life when his family is forced to leave their hometown and the traditions it holds.

While traditions can be good, they can sometimes trap us into a way of thinking or behaving that is contrary to God's will. In Colossians 2:8 Paul advises, "See to it that no one takes you captive through hollow and deceptive philosophy, which depends on human tradition and the basic principles of this world rather than on Christ" (NIV).

This week we see the Jewish Christians faced with a similar dilemma. Do they hold on to their religious tradition, allowing it to distort the gospel message, or do they lay aside customs and rituals and accept the gospel unaltered?

Connecting

As you open in prayer tonight, thank God for the insights that he has given you in this study.

1. Check in with your spiritual partner, or with another partner if yours is absent. Share your progress and any challenges you are currently facing. Take a few minutes to pray for each other now. Be sure to write down your partner's progress.

2. Share a tradition that has played a part in shaping your families' values.

Growing

Jesus was the Jewish Messiah, and his original disciples were all circumcised Jews who kept the Jewish law. When Gentiles came to faith in Jesus, many Jewish believers assumed that these Gentiles needed to be circumcised as Jews and keep the law too. They didn't see the law as an alternative to faith in Christ (faith vs. law); rather, they saw the law as the correct response to faith (faith plus law).

However, when Jewish Christians in the city of Antioch reached out to Gentiles, they told Gentile converts that they didn't have to become Jews in order to follow Christ. Saul/Paul was one of the leaders in Antioch who taught this new view. He said Jesus had fulfilled the Jewish law, and now the law was a cultural option, not the required response to faith.

For believers in Judea and Jerusalem, this was an outrageous idea. So the apostles and elders invited Paul, Barnabas, and other leaders from Antioch to Jerusalem to discuss and resolve this debate. Their meeting is called the Jerusalem Council.

Read Acts 11:19–30.

3. After the stoning of Stephen in Acts 2, some of the scattered believers went to Antioch and began preaching to Greeks (Gentiles) who believed and turned to the Lord (11:19–20). Why was their preaching so successful (v. 21)? Why do you believe this was significant?

4. When news of the growing church in Antioch reached Jerusalem, Barnabas, empowered by the Holy Spirit, went to encourage the Antioch church. Later, he and Saul (11:25–26) were leaders in the church and helped it grow. What encouragement and support did they offer the Antioch church?

Read Acts 15:1–21.

5. The Jewish believers from Judea in 15:1 are often called Judaizers, because they taught that Gentile converts had to become Jewish in order to follow Christ fully. Why might this have made sense to them?

6. Describe the process by which the believers sought to resolve this very difficult issue.

7. What reasons did Peter give for accepting the Gentiles without making them convert to Judaism (15:8–11)?

8. As a respected and well-respected Jewish elder, James (not the same James from 12:1) proposed a verdict in response to the evidence the council considered (vv. 19–21). What did he propose, and why?

9. In 1 Corinthians 8:9–13, Paul comments on one of these regulations. What insight do these verses give into why the Jerusalem Council decided these things were not allowed?

10. A letter confirming the council's decision was written and delivered to the Gentile churches (15:22–29). Why do you

think the Gentiles found the decision in the letter encouraging (15:30–31)?

11. Have you or someone you know ever altered or misrepresented the gospel out of a desire to hold on to some tradition or favorite practice? If so, what was the tradition or practice?

At the Jerusalem Council, the church confirmed that Gentiles were saved by grace and did not have to become Jews (through circumcision and keeping the law) in order to be acceptable to God.

Developing

By this point in the study, hopefully you've developed some new growth disciplines such as accountability, Scripture memorization, meditation on the Word of God, and prayer. Consider taking your commitment to know God better one step further.

12. If you've been spending time with God each day, consider journaling as a way to grow even closer to God. Read through *Journaling 101* found in the *Appendix*. Commit this week to spending a portion of your time with God writing your thoughts and prayers in a journal.

13. Briefly discuss the future of your group. How many of you are willing to stay together as a group and work through another study together? If you have time, turn to the *Small Group Agreement* and talk about any changes you would like to make as you move forward as a group.

Sharing

First Peter 5:2 says, "Be shepherds of God's flock" (NIV). A shepherd is one who cares for and guides people. When you help another believer grow in his or her relationship with Christ, when you truly listen to them with a loving heart, when you protect them from the world's lies and bring them to places where they can be fed, you are acting as their shepherd.

14. On your *Personal Health Plan*, next to the "Sharing" icon, answer the "WHEN are you shepherding another person in Christ?" question.

Surrendering

15. During the past two weeks, you've been praying for the specific needs of each person or couple in the group during the Circle of Prayer exercise. Take some time now to pray over those for whom the group hasn't yet prayed. As you did last week, allow each individual to share the specific needs or challenges they are facing. Ask for God's transforming power to bring change to their lives.

16. Don't forget to share your praises and prayer requests with one another and conclude your group time in prayer.

Before We Meet Again

In *Session Seven*, we will be discussing Acts chapters 20 through 26. Although questions will target specific passages, it is important that you understand the context of the passages we will be studying. With this in mind, read these chapters before meeting for *Session Seven*.

Study Notes

Believers who belonged to the party of the Pharisees: Because of their scrupulous keeping of the law, Pharisees who became followers of Jesus the Messiah may have had a greater tendency toward legalism with reference to Gentile Christians. The term "Judaizers" is often used of Jewish Christians who tried to force non-Jewish believers to adopt the hallmarks of Judaism—circumcision, dietary laws, rest on the Sabbath, etc.—in order to be fully acceptable to God.

Jerusalem Council: A conference held in about AD 49 between delegates from the church at Antioch of Syria and delegates from the church at Jerusalem. This council met to settle a dispute over whether Gentile converts to Christianity first had to identify with Judaism by being circumcised.

For Deeper Study (Optional)

Read Romans 3:9–31. What does this passage teach us about the relationships between:

1. Righteousness and sin?
2. Sin and the law?
3. The law and faith?
4. Faith and righteousness?

Reflections

J. Hudson Taylor once said, "Do not have your concert first, and then tune your instruments afterwards. Begin the day with the Word of God and prayer, and get first of all into harmony with Him."* Get into harmony with God as you spend time with him this week. Read and reflect on the daily verses. Then record your thoughts, insights, or prayers in the Reflect sections that follow.

* Charlie Jones and Bob Kelly, *The Tremendous Power of Prayer: A Collection of Quotes and InspirationalThoughts to Inspire Your Prayer Life* (West Monroe, LA: Howard Books, 2000).

On the sixth day record your summary of what God has taught you this week.

Day 1. I am not ashamed of the gospel, because it is the power of God for the salvation of everyone who believes: first for the Jew, then for the Gentile. For in the gospel a righteousness from God is revealed, a righteousness that is by faith from first to last, just as it is written: "The righteous will live by faith" (Rom. 1:16–17 NIV).

REFLECT

_____

_____

_____

_____

Day 2. God, who knows the heart, showed that he accepted them by giving the Holy Spirit to them, just as he did to us. He made no distinction between us and them, for he purified their hearts by faith (Acts 15:8–9 NIV).

REFLECT

_____

_____

_____

_____

Day 3. For it is by grace you have been saved, through faith—and this not from yourselves, it is the gift of God—not by works, so that no one can boast (Eph. 2:8–9 NIV).

REFLECT

_____

_____

_____

_____

Day 4. So too, at the present time there is a remnant chosen by grace. And if by grace, then it is no longer by works; if it were, grace would no longer be grace (Rom. 11:5–6 NIV).

REFLECT

_____

_____

_____

_____

Day 5. See to it that no one takes you captive through hollow and deceptive philosophy, which depends on human tradition and the basic principles of this world rather than on Christ (Col. 2:8 NIV).

REFLECT

_____

_____

_____

_____

Day 6. Record your summary of what God has taught you this week.

SUMMARY

_____

_____

_____

_____

PRISON EVANGELISM
THE GOSPEL IS NOT BOUND

Memory Verse: Now I want you to know, brothers, that what has happened to me has really served to advance the gospel (Phil. 1:12 NIV).

Jeremiah, a fiery preacher of righteousness, was called by God to be a prophet to the nations (Jer. 1:5). His primary message to the kingdom of Judah who had forsaken the Lord was one of repentance or certain destruction. Because of the nature of his message, he often endured captivity and physical acts of violence against him. In Jeremiah 20:8 he says, "Whenever I speak, I cry out proclaiming violence and destruction. So the word of the LORD has brought me insult and reproach all day long" (NIV). Try as they might, his persecutors could not extinguish the fire within him. He says in Jeremiah 20:9, "But if I say, 'I will not mention him or speak any more in his name,' his word is in my heart like a fire, a fire shut up in my bones. I am weary of holding it in; indeed, I cannot" (NIV). Ever conscious of his call, the Lord's message is carried out, even in the face of persecution and imprisonment.

All over the world today Christians are persecuted and imprisoned for the Lord's message. In spite of their oppressors' intentions, their incarceration does not confine their message; rather it fans the flame of God's Word within them so that they cry out like Jeremiah, "indeed, I cannot" hold it in.

Connecting

Open your group with prayer. Pray for God to embolden each of us in our faith and willingness to display it through our words and actions.

1. Check in with your spiritual partner, or with another partner if yours is absent. Share your progress and any challenges you are currently facing. Take a few minutes to pray for each other now. Be sure to write down your partner's progress.

2. Discuss Colossians 2:8. "See to it that no one takes you captive through hollow and deceptive philosophy, which depends on human tradition and the basic principles of this world rather than on Christ" (NIV). What does this reinforce from last week's study about what it takes to be saved?

Growing

Acts 13–14, 16–20 follow Paul as he takes the news of Jesus Christ around the Mediterranean world. In Acts 21 he arrives in Jerusalem at the end of his third missionary journey. He comes to deliver a donation of money from Gentile believers to impoverished Jewish believers, a practical expression of oneness in Christ despite cultural differences.

Paul's views on the Jewish law have not made him popular in Jerusalem. Rumor has it that he teaches Jews to forsake their heritage. James and the other Jewish Christian leaders propose that Paul demonstrate his support for Jewishness by joining in the purification rites of four men finishing a Nazarite vow. The plan goes bad when some Jews from Asia (in what is now Turkey) accuse Paul of teaching against the law.

3. Read Acts 21:17–26. Why do the leading believers in Jerusalem ask Paul to join in these Jewish purification rites?

4. What does Paul's willingness to participate in Jewish rites say about his view of the Jewish law?

5. Accusations are leveled at Paul (21:27–32). What are the charges? From what you know of Paul, how accurate are the charges?

6. Paul wants to speak to the crowd before being carried into the barracks. Read 21:37–22:22. What does he say in 22:21 to further enrage the crowd? Why do his words enrage them?

7. Why does Paul's announcement of his citizenship (22:23–29) stop the flogging from proceeding?

8. Read 23:1–11. Paul splits the Sanhedrin by presenting himself as a Pharisee and claiming that the central issue of his trial is resurrection. Why does this tactic work?

9. Read 23:12–35. Summarize the threats to Paul's life and how he escapes them.

10. Charges are brought against Paul before Governor Felix, and after two years of Paul's imprisonment without trial, Governor Festus takes over. Paul is asked to give his defense (25:8–12). Why do you think Paul exercises his right as a Roman citizen to appeal to Caesar's court in Rome, rather than being tried in Jerusalem?

11. Festus consults with the Jewish king Herod Agrippa II about Paul's case. Agrippa asks to hear Paul himself. What is his finding in 26:32?

Do you think Luke wants readers to think that Paul made a mistake by appealing to Caesar? Please explain your view.

12. Jesus's words in Luke 21:12–15 come to life through Paul's situation. Read the passage below and discuss how God's plan has been fulfilled through the events of this session.

    "But before all this, they will lay hands on you and persecute you. They will deliver you to synagogues and prisons, and you will be brought before kings and governors, and all on account of my name. This will result in your being witnesses to them. But make up your mind not to worry beforehand how you will defend yourselves. For I will give you words and wisdom that none of your adversaries will be able to resist or contradict" (Luke 21:12–15 NIV).

13. Before the trip to Jerusalem that set the events of Acts 20–26 in motion, Paul said, "And now, compelled by the Spirit, I am going to Jerusalem, not knowing what will happen to me there. I only know that in every city the Holy Spirit warns me that prison and hardships are facing me. However, I consider my life worth nothing to me, if only I may finish the race and complete the task the Lord Jesus has given me—the task of testifying to the gospel of God's grace" (Acts 20:22–24 NIV). How do you respond to Paul's attitude toward suffering for the gospel?

Although Paul is arrested in Jerusalem on false charges, held prisoner for two years in Caesarea, and heads to Rome under guard, the gospel is not bound by his chains and continues to advance according to God's plan.

 Developing

Jesus lived his life in service to God and others. In John 13:15, Jesus instructed his apostles to follow his example, saying, "I have set you an example that you should do as I have done for you" (NIV). Not only did Jesus tell us to serve one another, he empowered us with the gifts of the Holy Spirit. During this study, we've talked a lot about serving others using the gifts that God has given each of us. If we desire to live following Jesus's example, we must embrace our gifts and learn to serve as the Holy Spirit leads us.

14. First Corinthians 12:7 says, "A spiritual gift is given to each of us as a means of helping the entire church" (NLT). Review the *Spiritual Gifts Inventory* in the *Appendix* once again. As you read through the different gifts, make a star or check mark next to those that you think you have. If you haven't already done so, share what you believe your spiritual gifts are. If you have discovered a ministry in which to serve, share where you found the opportunities to exercise your gift(s), either within the small group, or in your church. This could serve as encouragement to those who are struggling to find a ministry.

   If you know your gifts but have not yet plugged into a ministry, discuss how your gifts might meet a need within your church. Make a commitment to take the necessary steps to get plugged into that ministry. Or if your group is continuing beyond this study of Acts, choose an area to begin serving within the small group.

   If you still do not know what your spiritual gift(s) are, review the inventory with a trusted friend who knows you well. Chances are they have witnessed one or more of these gifts in your life.

Sharing

Jesus's final command to his disciples was to be [his] witnesses in Jerusalem, and in all Judea and Samaria, and to the ends of the earth (Acts 1:8 NIV). Jesus wanted his disciples to share his gospel not only with their local communities but also the world. You can be involved in taking the gospel to all nations too.

15. Paul's ministry set in motion this final piece of Jesus's mandate to take the gospel to the ends of the earth. This mandate, as we have discussed, is for all of us as Jesus's followers. Prayerfully consider the following actions as a first step toward fulfilling Jesus's commission in your life.

☐ Hang a world map in the place where you pray at home. Pray for the world, then each continent, and then each country as the Lord leads you. Another way to pray for the world is to pray for the countries printed on your clothing labels as you get dressed each day.

☐ Send financial support to a missionary in a foreign country or a world mission's organization. To find a missionary to support, contact the Missions ministry of your church.

☐ Sponsor a child through a Christ-centered humanitarian aid organization.

16. During *Session Four* you discussed one tangible way to share Jesus in your "Judea and Samaria." If you brought items to donate tonight, spend a few minutes praying for the individuals or families who will receive them.

 ### Surrendering

Proverbs 3:5–6 says, "Trust in the LORD with all your heart and lean not on your own understanding; in all your ways acknowledge him, and he will make your paths straight" (NIV). Living a life of surrender means giving God your all—your past, your present, and your future. It involves offering your life daily to God through prayer, praise, and obedience to his Word, trusting in the Lord to guide us.

17. Turn to the *Personal Health Plan* and individually consider the "HOW are you surrendering your heart?" question. Look to the *Sample Personal Health Plan* for help. Share some of your thoughts with the group.

18. Share your prayer requests and record them on the *Prayer and Praise Report*. Have any previous prayer requests been answered? If so, celebrate these answers to prayer. Then, in simple, one-sentence prayers, submit your requests to God and close by thanking God for his commitment to your relationship with him and how he has used this group to teach you more about faith.

Study Notes

Nazarite Vow: A vow of consecration to the Lord (Num. 6:1–12).

Purification Rites: Rituals observed by Jews as a means of purifying oneself from ceremonial uncleanness, which prevented a person from entering the sanctuary. Uncleanness could be caused by things like contact with leprosy, a dead person, or in Paul's case, an extended stay in Gentile lands.

For Deeper Study (Optional)

As you read 2 Corinthians 6:4–10, reflect on what the apostles were willing to endure for the sake of the gospel.

> As servants of God we commend ourselves in every way: in great endurance; in troubles, hardships and distresses; in beatings, imprisonments and riots; in hard work, sleepless nights and hunger; in purity, understanding, patience and kindness; in the Holy Spirit and in sincere love; in truthful speech and in the power of God; with weapons of righteousness in the right hand and in the left; through glory and dishonor, bad report and good report; genuine, yet regarded as impostors; known, yet regarded as unknown; dying, and yet we live on; beaten, and yet not killed; sorrowful, yet always rejoicing; poor, yet making many rich; having nothing, and yet possessing everything (2 Cor. 6:4–10 NIV).

Reflections

As you read the given verse each day, prayerfully consider what you learn about God, his Spirit, and his place in your life. Then record your thoughts, insights, or prayer in the *Reflect* section below the verses you read. On the sixth day record a summary of what you have learned over the entire week through this study.

Day 1. However, I consider my life worth nothing to me, if only I may finish the race and complete the task the Lord Jesus has given me—the task of testifying to the gospel of God's grace (Acts 20:24 NIV).

REFLECT

_____
_____
_____
_____

Day 2. Yet when I preach the gospel, I cannot boast, for I am compelled to preach. Woe to me if I do not preach the gospel! If I preach voluntarily, I have a reward; if not voluntarily, I am simply discharging the trust committed to me (1 Cor. 9:16–17 NIV).

REFLECT

_____
_____
_____
_____

Day 3. We had previously suffered and been insulted in Philippi, as you know, but with the help of our God we dared to tell you his gospel in spite of strong opposition (1 Thess. 2:2 NIV).

REFLECT

_____
_____
_____
_____

Day 4. Then Paul answered, "Why are you weeping and breaking my heart? I am ready not only to be bound, but also to die in Jerusalem for the name of the Lord Jesus" (Acts 21:13 NIV).

REFLECT

_____

_____

_____

_____

Day 5. Consider him who endured such opposition from sinful men, so that you will not grow weary and lose heart (Heb. 12:3 NIV).

REFLECT

_____

_____

_____

_____

Day 6. Use the following space to summarize what God has revealed to you during *Session Seven* and the *Reflections*.

SUMMARY

_____

_____

_____

_____

TO ROME AND BEYOND
THE GOSPEL TO THE ENDS OF THE EARTH

Memory Verse: All over the world this gospel is bearing fruit and growing, just as it has been doing among you since the day you heard it and understood God's grace in all its truth (Col. 1:6 NIV).

Advances in communication have been astounding since the 1800s. The fastest communication available in 1840 was Samuel Morse's electric telegraph. The invention of the telephone followed in 1876; television broadcast began in 1930; computers were sold commercially in 1951; the fax was introduced in 1966; cellular phones were used in 1979; and the boundaryless World Wide Web was launched in 1999 making communication happen at light speed. New breakthroughs and discoveries are still happening today as we continue to demand more—faster.

With such global connectivity today, it's amazing that we haven't hastened the coming of the Lord by fulfilling his commission to go and make disciples of all nations (Matt. 28:19). Jesus said, "This gospel of the kingdom will be preached in the whole world as a testimony to all nations, and then the end will come" (Matt. 24:14 NIV).

There were already Christians in Rome by the time Paul arrived there under arrest, but he galvanized outreach in the city, and Luke uses his story as a model for the vision of global evangelization. We don't have to take a sea voyage to share the good news; in fact, we could transmit the gospel to astronauts on the moon. With communication technology literally at our fingertips, the potential to share the gospel is limitless.

Connecting

Several of you open your group with prayer, thanking God for what he has accomplished through this small group study.

1. Take time in this final session to connect with your spiritual partner. What has God been showing you through these sessions about the power of the Holy Spirit in the lives of believers? Check in with each other about the progress you have made in your spiritual growth during this study. Make plans about whether you will continue in your mentoring relationship outside your Bible study group.

2. Share one thing that you learned about yourself or God as a result of this study that you will begin to apply to your life.

Growing

After Paul's trial before King Herod Agrippa II, he sets sail for Rome. Once again, he faces difficulty but continues to share God's message of salvation boldly.
Read Acts 27:9–44.

3. Paul begins his journey to Rome but faces rough sailing conditions in October. Why don't the Roman officer and the ship's pilot heed his warning in 27:10?

4. In 27:21–26, just as the men have given up hope of surviving the storm, Paul speaks to them again about his earlier warning and then gives another prediction. What do you think is Paul's purpose for saying what he says?

   What is the men's response to Paul (vv. 30–32)?

5. With the storm still threatening to kill them all, how does Paul demonstrate his faith in Christ in 27:33–36?

6. When the ship finally runs aground, the soldiers plan to kill all of the prisoners (v. 42). This seems necessary because if the prisoners escape, the soldiers will pay with severe punishment—possibly their own lives. Why do you think the centurion wants to spare Paul's life (v. 43)?

Read Acts 28:1–30.

7. How do the events on the island of Malta further God's plan?

8. Who greets Paul en route to Rome in 28:14–15, and why is this noteworthy?

   How does Paul respond to the reception?

9. Under house arrest, Paul calls local Jewish leaders and defends himself to them in 28:17–20. What is their response (vv. 21–24)?

10. How does 28:25–27 summarize the Jewish response to the message of Christ?

    In Paul's view, what is the consequence of the Jewish response to the gospel (v. 28)?

11. Read Acts 28:30–31 and Philippians 1:12–14. According to these verses, how does Paul spend his time while under house arrest?

12. How does Paul's story affect you in your own walk with the Lord?

Despite extreme conditions, imprisonment, and threat of execution, the gospel of Jesus Christ cannot be chained. Paul continued to boldly proclaim God's message of salvation wherever he went, and the gospel advanced to Rome and even to Caesar himself.

Developing

13. If your group still needs to make decisions about continuing to meet after this session, have that discussion now. Talk about what you will study, who will lead, and where and when you will meet.

    Review your *Small Group Agreement* and evaluate how well you met your goals. Discuss any changes you want to make as you move forward. As your group starts a new study, this is a great time to take on a new role or change roles of service in your group. What new role will you take on? If you are uncertain, maybe your group members have some ideas for you. Remember you aren't making a lifetime commitment to the new role; it will only be for a few weeks. Maybe someone would like to share a role with you if you don't feel ready to serve solo.

Sharing

First Peter 3:15 says, "But in your hearts set apart Christ as Lord. Always be prepared to give an answer to everyone who asks you to give the reason for the hope that you have" (NIV). As this Scripture tells us, we should always be prepared to give an answer for the hope that we have found in Christ.

14. During the course of this study, you have made commitments to share Jesus with the people in your life, either by inviting your friends to grow in Christian community or by sharing

the gospel in words or actions with unbelievers. Share with the group any highlights that you experienced as you stepped out in faith to share with others.

 Surrendering

15. Take a couple of minutes to review the praises you have recorded over the past few weeks on the *Prayer and Praise Report*. Close by praying over your prayer requests, thanking God for what he's done in your group during this study.

For Deeper Study (Optional)

Read Romans 10:9–15.

1. How does Romans 10:9–15 tell us one is saved?

2. Why does Paul distinguish a difference between being justified and being saved in verse 10?

3. Verses 14 and 15 tell us why believers must be sent to the ends of the earth to preach the gospel.

4. What insight does James 2:19 give into why both belief and confession might be required of a true saving faith?

Reread Acts 1:6–8.

1. What question do the apostles ask Jesus in verse 6 and how does he respond?

2. How are verses 7 and 8 interrelated?

3. How does Romans 10:9–15 bring further clarity into Jesus's mandate in Acts 1:8?

4. "And this gospel of the kingdom will be preached in the whole world as a testimony to all nations, and then the end will come" (Matt. 24:14). Considering Romans 10:9–15 and Acts 1:6–8, what does this verse suggest about believers' involvement in preaching the gospel today?

Reflections

As you read through this final week of *Reflections*, prayerfully consider what God is showing you about his character, the Holy Spirit, and how he wants you to grow and change. Then, write down your thoughts or prayers in the space provided. Don't let this concluding week of *Reflections* be your last. Commit to continue reading, reflecting, and meditating on the Word of God daily.

Day 1. All over the world this gospel is bearing fruit and growing, just as it has been doing among you since the day you heard it and understood God's grace in all its truth (Col. 1:6 NIV).

REFLECT

_____
_____
_____
_____

Day 2. However, I consider my life worth nothing to me, if only I may finish the race and complete the task the Lord Jesus has given me—the task of testifying to the gospel of God's grace (Acts 20:24 NIV).

REFLECT

_____
_____

_____
_____

Day 3. Yet when I preach the gospel, I cannot boast, for I am compelled to preach. Woe to me if I do not preach the gospel! If I preach voluntarily, I have a reward; if not voluntarily, I am simply discharging the trust committed to me (1 Cor. 9:16–17 NIV).

REFLECT

_____
_____
_____
_____

Day 4. He said to them: "It is not for you to know the times or dates the Father has set by his own authority. But you will receive power when the Holy Spirit comes on you; and you will be my witnesses in Jerusalem, and in all Judea and Samaria, and to the ends of the earth" (Acts 1:7–8 NIV).

REFLECT

_____
_____
_____
_____

Day 5. And this gospel of the kingdom will be preached in the whole world as a testimony to all nations, and then the end will come (Matt. 24:14 NIV).

REFLECT

_____
_____

_____

_____

Day 6. Use the following space to write your prayer of commitment to continue spending time daily in God's Word and prayer.

SUMMARY

_____

_____

_____

_____

FREQUENTLY ASKED QUESTIONS

What do we do on the first night of our group?

Like all fun things in life—have a party! A "get to know you" coffee, dinner, or dessert is a great way to launch a new study. You may want to review the *Small Group Agreement* and share the names of a few friends you can invite to join you. But most importantly, have fun before your study time begins.

Where do we find new members for our group?

This can be challenging, especially for new groups that have only a few people or for existing groups that lose a few people along the way. We encourage you to pray with your group and then brainstorm a list of people from work, church, your neighborhood, your children's school, family, the gym, and so forth. Then have each group member invite several of the people on his or her list. Another good strategy is to ask church leaders to make an announcement that your group is open to new members.

No matter how you find members, it's vital that you stay on the lookout for new people to join your group. All groups tend to go through healthy attrition—the result of moves, releasing new leaders, ministry opportunities, and so forth—and if the group gets too small, it could be at risk of shutting down. If you and your group stay open, you'll be amazed at the people God sends your way. The next person just might become a friend for life. You never know!

How long will this group meet?

It's totally up to the group—once you come to the end of this study. Most groups meet weekly for at least their first six months together, but every other week can work as well. We strongly recommend that the group meet for the first six months on a weekly basis if at all possible. This allows for continuity, and if people miss a meeting they aren't gone for a whole month.

At the end of this study, each group member may decide whether he or she wants to continue on for another study. Some groups launch relationships that last for years, and others are stepping-stones into another group experience. Either way, enjoy the journey.

What if this group is not working for me?

Personality conflicts, life stage differences, geographical distance, level of spiritual maturity, or any number of things can cause you to feel the group doesn't work for you. Relax. Pray for God's direction, and at the end of this study decide whether to continue with this group or find another. You don't buy the first car you look at or marry the first person you date, and the same goes with a group. Don't bail out before the study is finished—God might have something to teach you. Also, don't run from conflict or prejudge people before you have given them a chance. God is still working in you too!

Who is the leader?

Most groups have an official leader. But ideally, the group will mature and members will share the facilitation of meetings. We have discovered that healthy groups share hosting and leading of the group. This model ensures that all members grow, give their unique contribution, and develop their gifts. This study guide and the Holy Spirit can keep things on track even when you share leadership. Christ has promised to be in your midst as you gather. Ultimately, God is your leader each step of the way.

How do we handle the child care needs in our group?

This can be a sensitive issue. We suggest that you empower the group to openly brainstorm solutions. You may try one option that works for a while and then adjust over time. Our favorite approach is for adults to meet in the living room or dining room, and share the cost of a babysitter (or two) who can be with the kids in a different part of the house. In this way, parents don't have to be away from their children all evening when their children are too young to be left at home. A second option is to use one home for the kids and a second home (close by) for the adults. A third idea is to rotate the responsibility of providing a lesson or care for the children either in the same home or in another home nearby. This can be an incredible blessing for kids. Finally, the most common idea is to decide that you need to have a night to invest in your spiritual lives individually or as a couple, and make your own arrangements for child care. No matter what decision the group makes, the best approach is to dialogue openly about both the problem and the solution.

SMALL GROUP AGREEMENT

Our Purpose

To transform our spiritual lives by cultivating our spiritual health in a healthy small group community. In addition, we:

_____

_____

_____

Our Values

Group Attendance	To give priority to the group meeting. We will call or e-mail if we will be late or absent. (Completing the *Small Group Calendar* will minimize this issue.)
Safe Environment	To help create a safe place where people can be heard and feel loved. (Please, no quick answers, snap judgments, or simple fixes.)
Respect Differences	To be gentle and gracious to people with different spiritual maturity, personal opinions, temperaments, or imperfections. We are all works in progress.
Confidentiality	To keep anything that is shared strictly confidential and within the group, and avoid sharing improper information about those outside the group.
Encouragement for Growth	To be not just takers but givers of life. We want to spiritually multiply our lives by serving others with our God-given gifts.

Welcome for Newcomers	To keep an open chair and share Jesus's dream of finding a shepherd for every sheep.
Shared Ownership	To remember that every member is a minister and to ensure that each attender will share a small team role or responsibility over time. (See the *Team Roles*.)
Rotating Hosts/ Leaders and Homes	To encourage different people to host the group in their homes, and to rotate the responsibility of facilitating each meeting. (See the *Small Group Calendar*.)

Our Expectations

- Refreshments/mealtimes _____
- Child care _____
- When we will meet (day of week) _____
- Where we will meet (place) _____
- We will begin at (time) _____ and end at _____
- We will do our best to have some or all of us attend a worship service together. Our primary worship service time will be _____
- Date of this agreement _____
- Date we will review this agreement again _____
- Who (other than the leader) will review this agreement at the end of this study _____

TEAM ROLES

The Bible makes clear that every member, not just the small group leader, is a minister in the body of Christ. In a healthy small group, every member takes on some small role or responsibility. It can be more fun and effective if you team up on these roles.

Review the team roles and responsibilities below, and have each member volunteer for a role or participate on a team. If someone doesn't know where to serve or is holding back, as a group, suggest a team or role. It's best to have one or two people on each team so you have each of the five purposes covered. Serving in even a small capacity will not only help your leader but also will make the group more fun for everyone. Don't hold back. Join a team!

The opportunities below are broken down by the five purposes and then by a *crawl* (beginning), *walk* (intermediate), or *run* (advanced) role. Try to cover at least the crawl and walk roles, and select a role that matches your group, your gifts, and your maturity.

Team Roles	Team Player(s)
CONNECTING TEAM (Fellowship and Community Building)	
Crawl: Host a social event or group activity in the first week or two.	_____
Walk: Create a list of uncommitted friends and then invite them to an open house or group social.	_____
Run: Plan a twenty-four-hour retreat or weekend getaway for the group. Lead the *Connecting* time each week for the group.	_____ _____
GROWING TEAM (Discipleship and Spiritual Growth)	
Crawl: Coordinate the spiritual partners for the group. Facilitate a three- or four-person discussion circle during the Bible study portion of your meeting. Coordinate the discussion circles.	_____ _____
Walk: Tabulate the *Personal Health Plans* in a summary to let people know how you're doing as a group. Encourage personal devotions through group discussions and pairing up with spiritual (accountability) partners.	_____ _____
Run: Take the group on a prayer walk, or plan a day of solitude, fasting, or personal retreat.	
SERVING TEAM (Discovering Your God-Given Design for Ministry)	
Crawl: Ensure that every member finds a group role or team he or she enjoys.	_____
Walk: Have every member take a gift test and determine your group's gifts. Plan a ministry project together.	_____ _____
Run: Help each member decide on a way to use his or her unique gifts somewhere in the church.	_____
SHARING TEAM (Sharing and Evangelism)	
Crawl: Coordinate the group's *Prayer and Praise Report* of friends and family who don't know Christ.	_____
Walk: Search for group mission opportunities and plan a cross-cultural group activity.	_____
Run: Take a small group "vacation" to host a six-week group in your neighborhood or office. Then come back together with your current group.	_____ _____
SURRENDERING TEAM (Surrendering Your Heart to Worship)	
Crawl: Maintain the group's *Prayer and Praise Report* or journal.	_____
Walk: Lead a brief time of worship each week (at the beginning or end of your meeting).	_____
Run: Plan a more unique time of worship.	_____

91

SMALL GROUP CALENDAR

Planning and calendaring can help ensure the greatest participation at every meeting. At the end of each meeting, review this calendar. Be sure to include a regular rotation of host homes and leaders, and don't forget birthdays, socials, church events, holidays, and mission/ministry projects.

Date	Lesson	Dessert/Meal	Role

PERSONAL HEALTH ASSESSMENT

	Just Beginning	Getting Going	Well Developed

CONNECTING with God's Family

I am deepening my understanding of and friendship with God in community with others.	1 2 3 4 5
I am growing in my ability both to share and to show my love to others.	1 2 3 4 5
I am willing to share my real needs for prayer and support from others.	1 2 3 4 5
I am resolving conflict constructively and am willing to forgive others.	1 2 3 4 5
CONNECTING Total	_____

GROWING to Be Like Christ

I have a growing relationship with God through regular time in the Bible and in prayer (spiritual habits).	1 2 3 4 5
I am experiencing more of the characteristics of Jesus Christ (love, patience, gentleness, courage, self-control, etc.) in my life.	1 2 3 4 5
I am avoiding addictive behaviors (food, television, busyness, and the like) to meet my needs.	1 2 3 4 5
I am spending time with a Christian friend (spiritual partner) who celebrates and challenges my spiritual growth.	1 2 3 4 5
GROWING Total	_____

93

	Just Beginning	Getting Going	Well Developed

DEVELOPING Your Gifts to Serve Others

I have discovered and am further developing my unique God-given design.   1 2 3 4 5

I am regularly praying for God to show me opportunities to serve him and others.   1 2 3 4 5

I am serving in a regular (once a month or more) ministry in the church or community.   1 2 3 4 5

I am a team player in my small group by sharing some group role or responsibility.   1 2 3 4 5

DEVELOPING Total   _____

SHARING Your Life Mission Every Day

I am cultivating relationships with non-Christians and praying for God to give me natural opportunities to share his love.   1 2 3 4 5

I am praying and learning about where God can use me and our group cross-culturally for missions.   1 2 3 4 5

I am investing my time in another person or group who needs to know Christ.   1 2 3 4 5

I am regularly inviting unchurched or unconnected friends to my church or small group.   1 2 3 4 5

SHARING Total   _____

SURRENDERING Your Life for God's Pleasure

I am experiencing more of the presence and power of God in my everyday life.   1 2 3 4 5

I am faithfully attending services and my small group to worship God.   1 2 3 4 5

I am seeking to please God by surrendering every area of my life (health, decisions, finances, relationships, future, etc.) to him.   1 2 3 4 5

I am accepting the things I cannot change and becoming increasingly grateful for the life I've been given.   1 2 3 4 5

SURRENDERING Total   _____

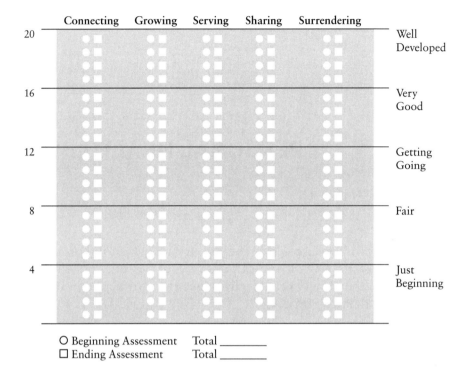

	Connecting	Growing	Serving	Sharing	Surrendering	
20						Well Developed
16						Very Good
12						Getting Going
8						Fair
4						Just Beginning

O Beginning Assessment   Total _____
□ Ending Assessment   Total _____

PERSONAL HEALTH PLAN

This worksheet could become your single most important feature in this study. On it you can record your personal priorities before the Father. It will help you live a healthy spiritual life, balancing all five of God's purposes.

PURPOSE	PLAN
CONNECT	WHO are you connecting with spiritually?
GROW	WHAT is your next step for growth?
DEVELOP	WHERE are you serving?
SHARE	WHEN are you shepherding another in Christ?
SURRENDER	HOW are you surrendering your heart to God?

DATE	MY PROGRESS	PARTNER'S PROGRESS

DATE	MY PROGRESS	PARTNER'S PROGRESS

SAMPLE PERSONAL HEALTH PLAN

This worksheet could become your single most important feature in this study. On it you can record your personal priorities before the Father. It will help you live a healthy spiritual life, balancing all five of God's purposes.

PURPOSE	PLAN
CONNECT	WHO are you connecting with spiritually?
	Bill and I will meet weekly by e-mail or phone
GROW	WHAT is your next step for growth?
	Regular devotions or journaling my prayers 2×/week
DEVELOP	WHERE are you serving?
	Serving in children's ministry Go through GIFTS Assessment
SHARE	WHEN are you shepherding another in Christ?
	Shepherding Bill at lunch or hosting a starter group in the fall
SURRENDER	HOW are you surrendering your heart?
	Help with our teenager New job situation

DATE	MY PROGRESS	PARTNER'S PROGRESS
3/5	Talked during our group	Figured out our goals together
3/12	Missed our time together	Missed our time together
3/26	Met for coffee and review of my goals	Met for coffee
4/10	E-mailed prayer requests	Bill sent me his prayer requests
5/5	Great start on personal journaling	Read Mark 1–6 in one sitting!
5/12	Traveled and not doing well this week	Journaled about Christ as healer
5/26	Back on track	Busy and distracted; asked for prayer
6/1	Need to call Children's Pastor	
6/26	Group did a serving project together	Agreed to lead group worship
6/30	Regularly rotating leadership	Led group worship–great job!
7/5	Called Jim to see if he's open to joining our group	Wanted to invite somebody, but didn't
7/12	Preparing to start a group in fall	
7/30	Group prayed for me	Told friend something I'm learning about Christ
8/5	Overwhelmed but encouraged	Scared to lead worship
8/15	Felt heard and more settled	Issue with wife
8/30	Read book on teens	Glad he took on his fear

SPIRITUAL GIFTS INVENTORY

A spiritual gift is given to each of us as a means of helping the entire church.

1 Corinthians 12:7 (NLT)

A spiritual gift is a special ability, given by the Holy Spirit to every believer at their conversion. Although spiritual gifts are given when the Holy Spirit enters new believers, their use and purpose need to be understood and developed as we grow spiritually. A spiritual gift is much like a muscle; the more you use it, the stronger it becomes.

A Few Truths about Spiritual Gifts

1. Only believers have spiritual gifts. 1 Corinthians 2:14
2. You can't earn or work for a spiritual gift. Ephesians 4:7
3. The Holy Spirit decides what gifts I get. 1 Corinthians 12:11
4. I am to develop the gifts God gives me. Romans 11:29; 2 Timothy 1:6
5. It's a sin to waste the gifts God gave me. 1 Corinthians 4:1–2; Matthew 25:14–30
6. Using my gifts honors God and expands me. John 15:8

Gifts Inventory

God wants us to know what spiritual gift(s) he has given us. One person can have many gifts. The goal is to find the areas in which the Holy Spirit seems to have supernaturally empowered our service to others. These gifts are to be used to minister to others and build up the body of Christ.

There are four main lists of gifts found in the Bible in Romans 12:3–8; 1 Corinthians 12:1–11, 27–31; Ephesians 4:11–12; and 1 Peter 4:9–11. There are other passages that mention or illustrate gifts not included in these lists. As you read through this list, prayerfully consider whether the biblical definition describes you. Remember, you can have more than one gift, but everyone has at least one.

ADMINISTRATION (Organization)—1 Corinthians 12
This is the ability to recognize the gifts of others and recruit them to a ministry. It is the ability to organize and manage people, resources, and time for effective ministry.

APOSTLE—1 Corinthians 12
This is the ability to start new churches/ventures and oversee their development.

DISCERNMENT—1 Corinthians 12
This is the ability to distinguish between the spirit of truth and the spirit of error; to detect inconsistencies in another's life and confront in love.

ENCOURAGEMENT (Exhortation)—Romans 12
This is the ability to motivate God's people to apply and act on biblical principles, especially when they are discouraged or wavering in their faith. It is also the ability to bring out the best in others and challenge them to develop their potential.

EVANGELISM—Ephesians 4
This is the ability to communicate the gospel of Jesus Christ to unbelievers in a positive, nonthreatening way and to sense opportunities to share Christ and lead people to respond with faith.

FAITH—1 Corinthians 12

This is the ability to trust God for what cannot be seen and to act on God's promise, regardless of what the circumstances indicate. This includes a willingness to risk failure in pursuit of a God-given vision, expecting God to handle the obstacles.

GIVING—Romans 12

This is the ability to generously contribute material resources and/or money beyond the 10 percent tithe so that the church may grow and be strengthened. It includes the ability to manage money so it may be given to support the ministry of others.

HOSPITALITY—1 Peter 4:9–10

This is the ability to make others, especially strangers, feel warmly welcomed, accepted, and comfortable in the church family and the ability to coordinate factors that promote fellowship.

LEADERSHIP—Romans 12

This is the ability to clarify and communicate the purpose and direction ("vision") of a ministry in a way that attracts others to get involved, including the ability to motivate others, by example, to work together in accomplishing a ministry goal.

MERCY—Romans 12

This is the ability to manifest practical, compassionate, cheerful love toward suffering members of the body of Christ.

PASTORING (Shepherding)—Ephesians 4

This is the ability to care for the spiritual needs of a group of believers and equip them for ministry. It is also the ability to nurture a small group in spiritual growth and assume responsibility for their welfare.

PREACHING—Romans 12

This is the ability to publicly communicate God's Word in an inspired way that convinces unbelievers and both challenges and comforts believers.

SERVICE—Romans 12

This is the ability to recognize unmet needs in the church family, and take the initiative to provide practical assistance quickly, cheerfully, and without a need for recognition.

TEACHING—Ephesians 4

This is the ability to educate God's people by clearly explaining and applying the Bible in a way that causes them to learn; it is the ability to equip and train other believers for ministry.

WISDOM—1 Corinthians 12

This is the ability to understand God's perspective on life situations and share those insights in a simple, understandable way.

TELLING YOUR STORY

First, don't underestimate the power of your testimony. Revelation 12:11 says, "They have defeated [Satan] by the blood of the Lamb and by their testimony. And they did not love their lives so much that they were afraid to die" (NLT).

A simple three-point approach is very effective in communicating your personal testimony. The approach focuses on before you trusted Christ, how you surrendered to him, and the difference in you since you've been walking with him. If you became a Christian at a very young age and don't remember what life was like before Christ, reflect on what you have seen in the lives of others. Before you begin, pray and ask God to give you the right words.

Before You Knew Christ

Simply tell what your life was like before you surrendered to Christ. What was the key problem, emotion, situation, or attitude you were dealing with? What motivated you? What were your actions? How did you try to satisfy your inner needs? Create an interesting picture of your preconversion life and problems, and then explain what created a need and interest in Christian things.

How You Came to Know Christ

How were you converted? Simply tell the events and circumstances that caused you to consider Christ as the solution to your needs. Take time to identify the steps that brought you to the point of trusting Christ. Where were you? What was happening at the time? What people or problems influenced your decision?

The Difference Christ Has Made in Your Life

What is different about your life in Christ? How has his forgiveness impacted you? How have your thoughts, attitudes, and emotions changed? What problems have been resolved or changed? Share how Christ is meeting your needs and what a relationship with him means to you now. This should be the largest part of your story.

Tips

- Don't use jargon: don't sound churchy, preachy, or pious.
- Stick to the point. Your conversion and new life in Christ should be the main points.
- Be specific. Include events, genuine feelings, and personal insights, both before and after conversion, which people would be interested in and that clarify your main point. This makes your testimony easier to relate to. Assume you are sharing with someone with no knowledge of the Christian faith.
- Be current. Tell what is happening in your life with God now, today.
- Be honest. Don't exaggerate or portray yourself as living a perfect life with no problems. This is not realistic. The simple truth of what God has done in your life is all the Holy Spirit needs to convict someone of their sin and convince them of his love and grace.
- Remember, it's the Holy Spirit who convicts. You need only be obedient and tell your story.
- When people reply to your efforts to share with statements like "I don't believe in God," "I don't believe the Bible is God's Word," or "How can a loving God allow suffering?" how can we respond to these replies?

- Above all, keep a positive attitude. Don't be defensive.
- Be sincere. This will speak volumes about your confidence in your faith.
- Don't be offended. It's not you they are rejecting.
- Pray—silently on-the-spot. Don't proceed without asking for God's help about the specific question. Seek his guidance on how, or if, you should proceed at this time.
- In God's wisdom, choose to do one of the following:
  - Postpone sharing at this time.
  - Answer their objections, if you can.
  - Promise to research their questions and return answers later.

Step 1. Everywhere Jesus went he used stories, or parables, to demonstrate our need for salvation. Through these stories, he helped people see the error of their ways, leading them to turn to him. Your story can be just as powerful today. Begin to develop your story by sharing what your life was like before you knew Christ. (If you haven't yet committed your life to Christ, or became a Christian at a very young age and don't remember what life was like before Christ, reflect on what you have seen in the life of someone close to you.) Make notes about this aspect of your story below and commit to writing it out this week.

_____

_____

_____

Step 2. Sit in groups of two or three people for this discussion. Review the "How You Came to Know Christ" section. Begin to develop this part of your story by sharing within your circle. Make notes about this aspect of your story below and commit to writing it out this week.

_____

_____

_____

Step 2b. Connecting: Go around the group and share about a time you were stopped cold while sharing Christ, by a question you couldn't answer. What happened?

Step 2c. Sharing: Previously we talked about the questions and objections we receive that stop us from continuing to share our faith with someone. These questions/objections might include:

- "I don't believe in God."
- "I don't believe the Bible is God's Word."
- "How can a loving God allow suffering?"

How can we respond to these replies?

Step 3. Subgroup into groups of two or three people for this discussion. Review "The Difference Christ Has Made in Your Life" section. Share the highlights of this part of your story within your circle. Make notes about this aspect of your story below and commit to writing it out this week.

_____

_____

_____

Step 3b. Story: There's nothing more exciting than a brand-new believer. My wife became a Christian four years before I met her. She was a flight attendant at the time. Her zeal to introduce others to Jesus was reminiscent of the woman at the well who ran and got the whole town out to see Jesus.

My wife immediately began an international organization of Christian flight attendants for fellowship and for reaching out to others in their profession. She organized events where many people came to Christ, and bid for trips with another flight attendant who was a Christian so they could witness on the planes. They even bid for the shorter trips so they could talk to as many different people as possible. They had a goal for every flight to talk to at least one person about Christ, and to be encouraged by at least one person who already knew him. God met that request every time.

In her zeal, however, she went home to her family over the holidays and vacations and had little or no success. Later she would realize that she pressed them too hard. Jesus said a prophet is without honor in his own town, and I think the same goes for family. That's because members of your family think they know you, and are more likely to ignore changes, choosing instead to see you as they've always seen you. "Isn't this the carpenter's son—the son of Joseph?" they said of Jesus. "Don't we know this guy?"

With family members you have to walk with Christ openly and be patient. Change takes time. And remember, we don't save anyone. We just introduce them to Jesus through telling our own story. God does the rest.

Step 4. As a group, review *Telling Your Story*. Share which part of your story is the most difficult for you to tell. Which is the easiest for you? If you have time, a few of you share your story with the group.

Step 5. Throughout this study we have had the opportunity to develop our individual testimonies. One way your group can serve each other is to provide a safe forum for "practicing" telling your stories. Continue to take turns sharing your testimonies now. Set a time limit—say two to three minutes each. Don't miss this great opportunity to get to know one another better and encourage each other's growth too.

SERVING COMMUNION

Churches vary in their treatment of communion (or the Lord's Supper). We offer one simple form by which a small group can share this experience together. You can adapt this as necessary, or omit it from your group altogether, depending on your church's beliefs.

Steps in Serving Communion

1. Open by sharing about God's love, forgiveness, grace, mercy, commitment, tenderheartedness, faithfulness, etc., out of your personal journey (connect with the stories of those in the room).
2. Read one or several of the passages listed below.
3. Pray and pass the bread around the circle.
4. When everyone has been served, remind them that this represents Jesus's broken body on their behalf. Simply state, "Jesus said, 'Do this in remembrance of me' (Luke 22:19 NIV). Let us eat together," and eat the bread as a group.
5. Then read the rest of the passage: "In the same way, after the supper he took the cup, saying, 'This cup is the new covenant in my blood, which is poured out for you'" (Luke 22:20 NIV).
6. Pray, and serve the cups, either by passing a small tray, serving them individually, or having members pick up a cup from the table.
7. When everyone has been served, remind them the juice represents Christ's blood shed for them, then simply state, "Take and drink in remembrance of him. Let us drink together."
8. Finish by singing a simple song, listening to a praise song, or having a time of prayer in thanks to God.

Communion passages: Matthew 26:26–29; Mark 14:22–25; Luke 22:14–20; 1 Corinthians 10:16–21; 11:17–34.

PERFORMING A FOOTWASHING

Scripture: John 13:1–17. Jesus makes it quite clear to his disciples that his position as the Father's Son includes being a servant rather than power and glory only. To properly understand the scene and the intention of Jesus, we must realize that the washing of feet was the duty of slaves and indeed of non-Jewish rather than Jewish slaves. Jesus placed himself in the position of a servant. He displayed to the disciples self-sacrifice and love. In view of his majesty, only the symbolic position of a slave was adequate to open their eyes and keep them from lofty illusions. The point of footwashing, then, is to correct the attitude that Jesus discerned in the disciples. It constitutes the permanent basis for mutual service, service in your group and for the community around you, which is the responsibility of all Christians.

When to Implement

There are three primary places we would recommend you insert a footwashing: during a break in the Surrendering section of your group; during a break in the Growing section of your group; or at the closing of your group. A special time of prayer for each person as he or she gets his or her feet washed can be added to the footwashing time.

SURRENDERING AT THE CROSS

Surrendering everything to God is one of the most challenging aspects of following Jesus. It involves a relationship built on trust and faith. Each of us is in a different place on our spiritual journey. Some of us have known the Lord for many years, some are new in our faith, and some may still be checking God out. Regardless, we all have things that we still want control over—things we don't want to give to God because we don't know what he will do with them. These things are truly more important to us than God is—they have become our god.

We need to understand that God wants us to be completely devoted to him. If we truly love God with all our heart, soul, strength, and mind (Luke 10:27), we will be willing to give him everything.

Steps in Surrendering at the Cross

1. You will need some small pieces of paper and pens or pencils for people to write down the things they want to sacrifice/surrender to God.
2. If you have a wooden cross, hammers, and nails you can have the members nail their sacrifices to the cross. If you don't have a wooden cross, get creative. Think of another way to symbolically relinquish the sacrifices to God. You might use a fireplace to burn them in the fire as an offering to the Lord. The point is giving to the Lord whatever hinders your relationship with him.

3. Create an atmosphere conducive to quiet reflection and prayer. Whatever this quiet atmosphere looks like for your group, do the best you can to create a peaceful time to meet with God.

4. Once you are settled, prayerfully think about the points below. Let the words and thoughts draw you into a heart-to-heart connection with your Lord Jesus Christ.

   ☐ *Worship him.* Ask God to change your viewpoint so you can worship him through a surrendered spirit.

   ☐ *Humble yourself.* Surrender doesn't happen without humility. James 4:6–7 says: "'God opposes the proud but gives grace to the humble.' Submit yourselves, then, to God" (NIV).

   ☐ *Surrender your mind, will, and emotions.* This is often the toughest part of surrendering. What do you sense God urging you to give him so you can have the kind of intimacy he desires with you? Our hearts yearn for this kind of connection with him; let go of the things that stand between you.

   ☐ *Write out your prayer.* Write out your prayer of sacrifice and surrender to the Lord. This may be an attitude, a fear, a person, a job, a possession—anything that God reveals is a hindrance to your relationship with him.

5. After writing out your sacrifice, take it to the cross and offer it to the Lord. Nail your sacrifice to the cross, or burn it as a sacrifice in the fire.

6. Close by singing, praying together, or taking communion. Make this time as short or as long as seems appropriate for your group.

Surrendering to God is life-changing and liberating. God desires that we be overcomers! First John 4:4 says, "You, dear children, are from God and have overcome . . . because the one who is in you is greater than the one who is in the world" (NIV).

JOURNALING 101

Henri Nouwen says effective and lasting ministry *for* God grows out of a quiet place alone *with* God. This is why journaling is so important.

The greatest adventure of our lives is found in the daily pursuit of knowing, growing in, serving, sharing, and worshiping Christ forever. This is the essence of a purposeful life: to see all these biblical purposes fully formed and balanced in our lives. Only then are we "complete in Christ" (Col. 1:28 NASB).

David poured his heart out to God by writing psalms. The book of Psalms contains many of his honest conversations with God in written form, including expressions of every imaginable emotion on every aspect of his life. Like David, we encourage you to select a strategy to integrate God's Word and journaling into your devotional time. Use any of the following resources:

- Bible
- Bible reading plan
- Devotional
- Topical Bible study plan

Before and after you read a portion of God's Word, speak to God in honest reflection in the form of a written prayer. You may begin this time by simply finishing the sentence "Father, . . . ," "Yesterday, Lord, . . . ," or "Thank you, God, for, ..." Share with him where you are at the present moment; express your hurts, disappointments, frustrations, blessings, victories, and gratefulness. Whatever you do with your journal, make a plan that fits you, so you'll have a positive experience. Consider sharing highlights of your progress and experiences with some or all of your group members, especially your spiritual partner. You may find they want to join and even encourage you in this journey. Most of all, enjoy the ride and cultivate a more authentic, growing walk with God.

PRAYER AND PRAISE REPORT

Briefly share your prayer requests with the large group, making notations below. Then gather in small groups of two to four to pray for each other.

Date: _____

Prayer Requests

_____
_____
_____
_____
_____

Praise Reports

_____
_____
_____
_____
_____

Prayer and Praise Report

Briefly share your prayer requests with the large group, making notations below. Then gather in small groups of two to four to pray for each other.

Date: _____

Prayer Requests

_____
_____
_____
_____
_____

Praise Reports

_____
_____
_____
_____
_____

Prayer and Praise Report

Briefly share your prayer requests with the large group, making notations below. Then gather in small groups of two to four to pray for each other.

Date: _____

Prayer Requests

_____
_____
_____

_____

_____

Praise Reports

_____

_____

_____

_____

_____

Prayer and Praise Report

Briefly share your prayer requests with the large group, making notations below. Then gather in small groups of two to four to pray for each other.

Date: _____

Prayer Requests

_____

_____

_____

_____

_____

Praise Reports

_____

_____

_____

_____

_____

Prayer and Praise Report

Briefly share your prayer requests with the large group, making notations below. Then gather in small groups of two to four to pray for each other.

Date: _____

Prayer Requests

_____

_____

_____

_____

_____

Praise Reports

_____

_____

_____

_____

_____

SMALL GROUP ROSTER

Name	Address	Phone	E-mail Address	Team or Role	When/How to Contact You
Bill Jones	7 Alvalar Street L.F. 92665	766-2255	bjones@aol.com	Socials	Evenings After 5

(Pass your book around your group at your first meeting to get every-one's name and contact information.)

Name	Address	Phone	E-mail Address	Team or Role	When/How to Contact You

LEADING FOR THE FIRST TIME
LEADERSHIP 101

Sweaty palms are a healthy sign. The Bible says God is gracious to the humble. Remember who is in control; the time to worry is when you're not worried. Those who are soft in heart (and sweaty-palmed) are those whom God is sure to speak through.

Seek support. Ask your leader, coleader, or close friend to pray for you and prepare with you before the session. Walking through the study will help you anticipate potentially difficult questions and discussion topics.

Bring your uniqueness to the study. Lean into who you are and how God wants you to uniquely lead the study.

Prepare. Prepare. Prepare. Go through the session several times. If you are using the DVD, listen to the teaching segment and *Leader Lifter*. Consider writing in a journal or fasting for a day to prepare yourself for what God wants to do.

Don't wait until the last minute to prepare.

Ask for feedback so you can grow. Perhaps in an e-mail or on cards handed out at the study, have everyone write down three things you did well and one thing you could improve on. Don't get defensive, but show an openness to learn and grow.

Prayerfully consider launching a new group. This doesn't need to happen overnight, but God's heart is for this to happen over time. Not all Christians are called to be leaders or teachers, but we are all called to be "shepherds" of a few someday.

Share with your group what God is doing in your heart. God is searching for those whose hearts are fully his. Share your trials and victories. We promise that people will relate.

Prayerfully consider whom you would like to pass the baton to next week. It's only fair. God is ready for the next member of your group to go on the faith journey you just traveled. Make it fun, and expect God to do the rest.

LEADER'S NOTES
INTRODUCTION

Congratulations! You have responded to the call to help shepherd Jesus's flock. There are few other tasks in the family of God that surpass the contribution you will be making. We have provided you several ways to prepare for this role. Between the *Read Me First*, these *Leader's Notes*, and the *Watch This First* and *Leader Lifter* segments on the optional *Deepening Life Together: Acts* Video Teaching DVD, you'll have all you need to do a great job of leading your group. Just don't forget, you are not alone. God knew that you would be asked to lead this group and he won't let you down. In Hebrews 13:5b God promises us, "Never will I leave you; never will I forsake you" (NIV).

Your role as leader is to create a safe, warm environment for your group. As a leader, your most important job is to create an atmosphere where people are willing to talk honestly about what the topics discussed in this study have to do with them. Be available before people arrive so you can greet them at the door. People are naturally nervous at a new group, so a hug or handshake can help put them at ease. Before you start leading your group, a little preparation will give you confidence. Review the *Read Me First* at the front of your study guide so you'll understand the purpose of each section, enabling you to help your group understand it as well.

If you're new to leading a group, congratulations and thank you; this will be a life-changing experience for you also. We have provided these *Leader's Notes* to help new leaders begin well.

It's important in your first meeting to make sure group members understand that things shared personally and in prayer must remain confidential. Also, be careful not to dominate the group discussion, but facilitate it and encourage others to join in and share. And lastly, have fun.

Take a moment at the beginning of your first meeting to orient the group to one principle that undergirds this study: A healthy small group balances the purposes of the church. Most small groups emphasize Bible study, fellowship, and prayer. But God has called us to reach out to others as well. He wants us to do what Jesus teaches, not just learn about it.

Preparing for each meeting ahead of time. Take the time to review the session, the *Leader's Notes*, and *Leader Lifter* for the session before each session. Also write down your answers to each question. Pay special attention to exercises that ask group members to *do* something. These exercises will help your group live out what the Bible teaches, not just talk about it. Be sure you understand how the exercises work, and bring any supplies you might need, such as paper or pens. Pray for your group members by name at least once between sessions and before each session. Use the *Prayer and Praise Report* so you will remember their prayer requests. Ask God to use your time together to touch the heart of every person. Expect God to give you the opportunity to talk with those he wants you to encourage or challenge in a special way.

Don't try to go it alone. Pray for God to help you. Ask other members of your group to help by taking on some small role. In the *Appendix* you'll find the *Team Roles* pages with some suggestions to get people involved. Leading is more rewarding if you give group members opportunities to help. Besides, helping group members discover their individual gifts for serving or even leading the group will bless all of you.

Consider asking a few people to come early to help set up, pray, and introduce newcomers to others. Even if everyone is new, they don't know that yet and may be shy when they arrive. You might give people roles like setting up name tags or handing out drinks. This could be a great way to spot a co-leader.

Subgrouping. If your group has more than seven people, break into discussion groups of three to four people for the *Growing* and *Surrendering* sections each week. People will connect more with the study and each other when they have more opportunity to participate. Smaller discussion circles encourage quieter people to talk more and tend to minimize the effects of more vocal or dominant members. Also, people who are unaccustomed to praying aloud will feel more comfortable praying within a smaller group of people. Share prayer requests in the larger group and then break into smaller groups to pray for each other. People are more willing to pray in small circles if they know that the whole group will hear all the prayer requests.

Memorizing Scripture. At the start of each session you will find a memory verse—a verse for the group to memorize each week. Encourage your group members to do this. Memorizing God's Word is both directed and celebrated throughout the Bible, either explicitly ("Your word I have hidden in my heart, that I might not sin against You" [Ps. 119:11 NKJV]), or implicitly, as in the example of our Lord ("He departed to the mountain to pray" [Mark 6:46 NKJV]).

Anyone who has memorized Scripture can confirm the amazing spiritual benefits that result from this practice. Don't miss out on the opportunity to encourage your group to grow in the knowledge of God's Word through Scripture memorization.

Reflections. We've provided opportunity for a personal time with God using the *Reflections* at the end of each session. Don't press seekers to do this, but just remind the group that every believer should have a plan for personal time with God.

Inviting new people. Cast the vision, as Jesus did, to be inclusive not exclusive. Ask everyone to prayerfully think of people who would enjoy or benefit from a group like this—then invite them. The beginning of a new study is a great time to welcome a few people into your circle. Don't worry about ending up with too many people—you can always have one discussion circle in the living room and another in the dining room.

For Deeper Study (Optional). We have included a *For Deeper Study* section in each session. *For Deeper Study* provides additional passages for individual study on the topic of each session. If your group likes to do deeper Bible study, consider having members study the *For Deeper Study* passages for homework. Then, during the *Growing* portion of your meeting, you can share the high points of what you've learned.

LEADER'S NOTES
SESSIONS

Session One Brilliant Beginnings

Connecting

1. We've designed this study for both new and established groups, and for both seekers and the spiritually mature. New groups will need to invest more time building relationships with each other. Established groups often want to dig deeper into Bible study and application. Regardless of whether your group is new or has been together for a while, be sure to answer this introductory question at this first session.

2. A very important item in this first session is the *Small Group Agreement*. An agreement helps clarify your group's priorities and cast new vision for what the group can become. You can find this in the *Appendix* of this study guide. We've found that groups that talk about these values up front and commit to an agreement benefit significantly. They work through conflicts long before people get to the point of frustration, so there's a lot less pain.

   Take some time to review this agreement before your meeting. Then during your meeting, read the agreement aloud to the entire group. If some people have concerns about a specific item or the agreement as a whole, be sensitive to their concerns. Explain that tens of thousands of groups use agreements like this one as a simple tool for building trust and group health over time.

   We recommend talking about shared ownership of the group. It's important that each member have a role. See the *Appendix* to learn more about Team Roles. This is a great tool to get this important practice launched in your group.

   If your group is new, you may want to focus on welcoming newcomers or on sharing group ownership. Any group will quickly move from being the leader's group to our group if everyone understands the goals of the group and shares a small role. See the *Team Roles* in the *Appendix* for help on how to do this well.

Growing

Have someone read Bible passages aloud. It's a good idea to ask ahead of time, because not everyone is comfortable reading aloud in public.

4. The disciples will be witnesses—first locally and eventually globally—testifying to the events of Jesus's life, death, and resurrection. They will receive power to fulfill this mission when the Holy Spirit comes on them. The mission, its content and scope, and the source of the power to fulfill it are all key.

   The disciples should not just stand around looking up into the sky as though they are losing Jesus; they are to set about the mandate that Jesus gave them because no one knows the day or time that he will return. Believers today should also serve Christ while awaiting his return. The two men dressed in white were basically saying, "Don't just stand around reminiscing about what was; get busy!"

5. The promised gift was the empowering infilling of the Holy Spirit.

6. Peter used Scripture (Psalm 55:12–15) as a basis for replacing Judas Iscariot. By choosing twelve disciples, Jesus was symbolically replicating the twelve tribes of Israel. His twelve apostles symbolized the nation Israel, the faithful remnant of God's people.

7. The Jews were bewildered and amazed. Some questioned this demonstration of the power of the Holy Spirit, while others made fun of the disciples attributing their display to drunkenness.

   The resurrection is the evidence that Jesus is the Messiah promised in the Old Testament. If Jesus wasn't raised from the dead, then he was merely one of thousands of men crucified as criminals by the Romans. Lots of people saw Jesus before his death. The apostles were the witnesses who saw him alive after his death. This was an astounding claim to make, but the Holy Spirit's power backed up Peter's assertion.

8. The indwelling gift of the Spirit was and still is available to all who profess faith in Christ. People receive the Spirit at the moment of conversion.

9. The early church was devoted to the apostles' teaching, fellowship, breaking bread, prayer, and meeting the needs of the community. The teaching fed them with accurate knowledge of what Jesus did and taught, and what his death and resurrection meant. Fellowship went deeper than socializing—it fed the soul with shared life on an intimate and practical level. The breaking of bread involved shared meals that fed bodies and also the Lord's Supper,

which fed believers with a constant reminder of what Christ's broken body had done for them. Prayer taught them to talk and listen to God.

10. It is the power of the Holy Spirit that convicts souls and provokes belief.

11. The believers affirmed God's sovereign power in the face of the government's power. They petitioned the Lord for miraculous signs and wonders and for boldness in speaking his Word. After they prayed, the place they were praying in was shaken, they were filled with the Holy Spirit, and they spoke the Word of God boldly.

12. One receives the indwelling Spirit at conversion, one is continually filled with the Spirit, as Peter and John and the other believers were, by living consciously in the Lord's presence and allowing his Word and Spirit to dominate every aspect of our lives. Remaining filled with the Spirit (also referred to as walking in the Spirit) happens as we continually pursue godliness and righteous living, depending on his power to enable us.

13. Gamaliel said that if the apostles' activity was of human origin, then it would fail on its own, without influence of the Sanhedrin. If, however, the apostles' work was of God, then the Sanhedrin were powerless to stop them.

Developing

This section enables you to help the group see the importance of developing their abilities for service to God.

15. The intent of this discussion is to encourage group members to set aside some time to spend with God in prayer and his Word at home each day throughout the week. Read through this section and be prepared to help the group understand how important it is to fill our minds with the Word of God. If people already have a commitment to a good Bible reading plan, that is great, but you may have people who struggle to stay in the Word daily. Sometimes beginning with a simple commitment to a short daily reading can start a habit that changes their life.

The *Reflections* pages at the end of each session include verses that were either talked about in the session or support the teaching of the session. They are very short readings with a few lines to encourage people to write down their thoughts. Remind the group about these *Reflections* each week during the *Surrendering* section. Encourage the group to see the importance of making this time to connect with God a priority in their life. Offer further encouragement to commit to a next step in prayer, Bible reading, or meditation on the Word.

Suggested exercise: To help the group get started with meditating on the Word of God, provide everyone with a 3 × 5 index card. Have everyone write this week's memory verse on the card and begin memorizing Scripture together.

Surrendering

God is most pleased by a heart that is fully his. Each group session will provide group members a chance to surrender their hearts to God in prayer and worship. Group prayer requests and prayer time should be included every week.

18. Encourage group members to use the *Reflections* verses in their daily quiet time throughout the week. This will move them closer to God while reinforcing the lesson of this session through related Scripture.

19. As you move to a time of sharing prayer requests, be sure to remind the group of the importance of confidentiality and keeping what is shared in the group within the group. Everyone must feel that the personal things they share will be kept in confidence if you are to have safety and bonding among the group members.

Session Two Opposition and Expansion

Connecting

2. We encourage the group to rotate leaders and host homes each meeting. This practice will go a long way toward bonding the group. Review the *Small Group Calendar* and talk about who else is willing to open their home or facilitate a meeting. Rotating host homes and leadership along with implementing *Team Roles* as discussed in *Session One* will quickly move the group ownership from "the leader's group" to "our group."

Growing

4. There were two groups of Jews who made up the church at this point: the Greek-speaking (Hellenistic) Jews and the Hebrew or Aramaic-speaking Jews (see *Study Notes*). The Greek Jewish widows felt that they were not receiving an adequate share of the food that the church provided for their care. The apostles chose seven men from among the Greek Jews to fairly represent the Greeks' interests.

   The apostles' choosing of seven men from among the Greek Jews was a demonstration of love and unity. The apostles wanted the Greek Jews to feel their interests were represented fairly. Since the affairs of the church were in order, the apostles could then focus on the ministry of the gospel.

5. Stephen accused the Jewish leaders of being obstinate and behaving just as their ancestors had done in rejecting God's messengers. Now they had rejected and killed God's greatest messenger, the Righteous One, the Messiah himself.

6. The Sanhedrin responded in anger and frustration. Considering Stephen's message to be blasphemy, they imposed the punishment for blasphemy, which was stoning.

   Stephen spoke blessing over his persecutors as he prayed for the Lord to forgive them. As they were in the process of stoning Stephen, he made two statements, both reminiscent of Christ's words on the cross. "Lord Jesus, receive my spirit" is similar to Christ's final words in Luke 23:46 (in some manuscripts). The second is a request for forgiveness on behalf of his persecutors: "Lord, don't charge them with this sin!" (Luke 23:34). Stephen had obviously learned some important lessons from Jesus.

7. A great persecution broke out against the church of Jerusalem as a result of Stephen's stoning. The believers were scattered throughout the regions of Judea and Samaria preaching the gospel wherever they went. This marked the beginning of the fulfillment of Jesus's mandate in Acts 1:8: "But you will receive power when the Holy Spirit comes on you; and you will be my witnesses in Jerusalem, and in all Judea and Samaria, and to the ends of the earth" (NIV).

8. Evil spirits came out of many who were possessed. Paralytics and cripples were healed. Many believed and were baptized. And the gospel spread to Samaria. Philip's ministry is noteworthy for its miraculous elements, like Jesus's ministry.

   An angel directed Philip in a completely different direction, along the road to Gaza. On this road, he met an Ethiopian God-fearing non-Jew who had questions. Philip shared with him Jesus's fulfillment of the Isaiah 53 prophecy and baptized him. God was revealing his will for the church to spread beyond Jerusalem not only to Jews but to Samaritans (part-Jews) and Gentiles as well

Developing

10. For many, spiritual partners will be a new idea. We highly encourage you to try pairs for this study. It's so hard to start a spiritual practice like prayer or consistent Bible reading with no support. A friend makes a huge difference. As leader, you may want to prayerfully decide who would be a good match with whom. Remind people that this partnership isn't forever; it's just for a few weeks. Be sure to have extra copies of the *Personal Health Plan* available at this meeting in case you need to have a group of three spiritual partners.

It is a good idea for you to look over the *Personal Health Plan* before the meeting so you can help people understand how to use it.

Instruct your group members to enlist a spiritual partner by asking them to pair up with someone in the group (we suggest that men partner with men and women with women) and turn to the *Personal Health Plan* in the *Appendix*.

Ask the group to complete the instructions in the session for the WHO and WHAT questions on the *Personal Health Plan*. Your group has now begun to address two of God's purposes for their lives!

You can see that the *Personal Health Plan* contains space to record the ups and downs and progress each week in the column labeled "My Progress." When partners check in each week, they can record their partner's progress in the goal he or she chose in the "Partner's Progress" column on this chart. In the *Appendix* you'll find a *Sample Personal Health Plan* filled in as an example.

The WHERE, WHEN, and HOW questions on the *Personal Health Plan* will be addressed in future sessions of the study.

Sharing

12. A *Circles of Life* diagram is provided for you and the group to use to help you identify people who need a connection to Christian community. Encourage the group to commit to praying for God's guidance and an opportunity to reach out to each person in their *Circles of Life*.

    We encourage this outward focus for your group because groups that become too inwardly focused tend to become unhealthy over time. People naturally gravitate toward feeding themselves through Bible study, prayer, and social time, so it's usually up to the leader to push them to consider how this inward nourishment can overflow into outward concern for others. Never forget: Jesus came to seek and save the lost and to find a shepherd for every sheep.

    Talk to the group about the importance of inviting people; remind them that healthy small groups make a habit of inviting friends, neighbors, un-connected church members, co-workers, etc., to join their groups or join them at a weekend service. When people get connected to a group of new friends, they often join the church.

    Some groups are happy with the people they already have in the group and they don't really want to grow larger. Some fear that newcomers will interrupt the intimacy that members have built over time. However, groups generally gain strength with the infusion of new people. It's like a river of living water flowing into a stagnant pond. Some groups remain permanently open, while others open periodically, such as at the beginning and end of a study. If your circle becomes too large for easy face-to-face conversations, you can simply form a second or third discussion circle in another room in your home.

14. Last week we talked briefly about incorporating *Reflections* into the group members' daily time with God. Some people don't yet have an established quiet time. With this in mind, remind the group about the importance of making daily time with God a priority by simply reading aloud this item. Then talk about potential obstacles and practical ideas for overcoming them. The *Reflections* verses could serve as a springboard for drawing near to God. So don't forget these are a valuable resource for your group.

15. Be sure to remind the group of the importance of confidentiality and keeping what is shared in the group within the group. Use the *Prayer and Praise Report* in the *Appendix* to record your prayer requests.

Session Three A Persecutor Turns Apostle

Connecting

1. Encourage group members to take time to complete the *Personal Health Assessment* and pair up with their spiritual partner to discuss one thing that is going well and one thing that needs work. Participants should not be asked to share any aspect of this assessment in the large group if they don't want to.

Growing

3. The witnesses laying their clothes at the feet of Saul indicated that he was likely in charge of the execution.

4. Saul had murderous hatred for the Christians and was a leader of the persecution. According to 8:3, Saul began to destroy (NIV), or make havoc of (NKJV), the church, words that elsewhere are used of the ravages of wild animals or the total destruction of a city. This verse also says he went house to house and dragged believers off to prison.

5. Saul asked permission of the high priest to take prisoners from Damascus and transport them all the way to Jerusalem where they could be tried. As he traveled the road to Damascus, a light from heaven surrounded him and he heard a voice, identified as Jesus, question him on his reasons for persecuting Jesus. Saul was blinded, and Jesus sent him to Damascus with specific instructions on what to do next.

6. The voice from heaven and the bright light both suggested that this experience was from God. The Lord certainly went to extraordinary lengths to

change Saul's mind-set, but perhaps nothing less would have gotten through to a man with such a stubborn temperament.

7. Ananias was concerned because Saul had a reputation for harming believers. The Lord reassured him that he had a plan. Saul was God's chosen instrument to take the gospel to the Gentiles. This was as astonishing as Saul's conversion, as up to this point, with the exception of the Ethiopian, believers had assumed the gospel was for Jews only.

8. Saul's blindness distracted him from the world so he could focus on Christ for three days (as with Jonah's three days in the great fish). His blindness and then healing symbolized his spiritual blindness and then sudden revelation of the truth of the gospel.

9. His intellect and speaking skill must have been formidable, as many people were unable to answer his logic in demonstrating that Jesus was the Messiah. His passion must have been formidable too, and he aroused strong passions of rage in some and loyalty in others.

10. The believers had many reasons to fear Saul. Allow the group to openly discuss why they think fear was justified. It was Barnabas's testimony about the authenticity of Saul's conversion that finally convinced the believers to trust him.

11. Saul's dramatic conversion angered the unbelieving Jews because he had formerly persecuted the church alongside them. He may have seemed like more of a traitor.

12. The believers sent Saul to Tarsus because they did not want to further anger the Jews. They feared Saul's presence would provoke further persecution of the church, just as Stephen's death had done.

Developing

14. Group members who are currently serving the body of Christ in some capacity should be encouraged to share their experiences with the group as a way to encourage them. All group members should consider where they could take a next step toward getting involved in ministry. Discuss some of the ministries that your church may offer to people looking to get involved, such as the children's ministry, ushering, or hospitality. Remind everyone that it sometimes takes time and trying several different ministries before finding the one that fits best.

Sharing

15. It is important to return to the *Circles of Life* and encourage the group to follow through in their commitments to invite people who need to know Christ more deeply through Christian community. When people are asked why they never go to church, they often say, "No one ever invited me." Remind the group that our responsibility is to invite people, but it is the Holy Spirit's responsibility to compel them to come.

Surrendering

17. Allow everyone to share prayer requests as a group. Then encourage group members to pair up to pray for one another. When everyone has finished, invite one person to close the group time in prayer.

Session Four Into All the World

Growing

3. Cornelius was "God-fearing," which meant that he was a Gentile who had abandoned his pagan religion in favor of belief in the one, true God. Such God-fearers were not fully Jewish because they had not been circumcised and did not keep all of the Old Testament laws related to diet and ceremonial purity. He was also a centurion, a military officer with a regiment of fifty to a hundred men.

4. Cornelius was instructed to send men to retrieve Simon Peter from Joppa. He immediately obeyed.

5. Peter's vision established that God was making it possible to unite Gentiles with Jews, who had formerly been set apart. See *Study Notes* for more information.

6. Peter realized that God does not show favoritism to individuals on the basis of prestige, nationality, or wealth. This realization would destroy prejudice that may have prevented Peter from sharing the gospel with people of all races, nationalities, and stations in life.

7. The fact that Peter rather than Paul initiated the mission to the Gentiles is very important. Peter was highly respected among the Jewish followers of Christ, while Paul was suspect because he was a former persecutor. Peter's example would have more influence with the Jewish Christians.

8. The Jewish believers criticized him, accusing him of violating Jewish law by eating with the Gentiles who did not observe the laws regarding clean and unclean food. Even entering a Gentile home was considered unclean.

9. Peter quelled their objections by saying that the Holy Spirit came on Cornelius and his household. If God gave the Holy Spirit to Gentiles, how could the believers object? If they had continued their opposition, Christian faith would have remained a sect within Judaism rather than a worldwide movement.

Developing

11. Point the group to the *Spiritual Gifts Inventory* in the *Appendix*. Read through the spiritual gifts and engage the group in discussion about which gifts they believe they have. Encourage them to review these further on their own time during the coming week, giving prayerful consideration to each one. We will refer back to this again later in the study.

Sharing

12. This activity provides an opportunity for the group to share Jesus in a very practical way. Discuss this and choose one action step to take as a group. Be certain that everyone understands his or her role in this activity. It might be a good idea to call each person during the week to remind to bring to the next session what is required of them.

    Designate one person to investigate where to donate items in your area. That person can also be responsible for dropping off the items.

13. Encourage group members to consider developing their salvation story as a tool for sharing their faith with others. Begin the process during your group time and encourage the group to complete the exercise at home. As leader, you should review the "Tips" section of *Telling Your Story* yourself in advance and be ready to share your ideas about this process with the group.

Session Five Peter's Deliverance

Growing

4. Peter was guarded by four squads of four soldiers each. The four squads would probably have taken four different shifts, with two of the soldiers chained to Peter while the other two stood guard outside the cell door. This was a serious level of security.

    God always has the power to help us, so we should always pray and trust him. He won't always give us what we want—sometimes, as in James's case, his plan for the good of all people might even involve our suffering or death. Suffering is not a sign that God is absent, indifferent, powerless, or cruel. Suffering can be an opportunity to show that we love God no matter what.

5. Crises can destroy the church or it can strengthen it. Often, today we see church crises divide the church, but in this case, the believers came together as one to intercede on Peter's behalf.

6. The believers had been praying for Peter, yet they said, you're out of your mind when told Peter was at the door. Even though they had been earnestly praying for Peter, they apparently lacked faith that God would actually release him.

7. Herod made an exhaustive search for Peter and when his men didn't find him, he had the guards cross-examined and executed. At that time, the soldier or guard who was assigned to a prisoner would suffer the fate of the prisoner should they allow him to escape. Peter's escape was a serious challenge to Herod's authority and control.

8. God judged Herod with death because he accepted the acclaim that he was a god, refusing to give praise to God (Acts 12:23 NIV). Ultimately, this same judgment of death befalls all who refuse to give God praise. God's judgment on Herod could be seen as divine retribution for Herod's own judgment of death on James.

Developing

11. Encourage group members to use the *Personal Health Plan* to jot down their next step to serving in ministry, with a plan for how and when they will begin.

Session Six Tradition Challenges Innovation

Growing

3. They were successful because the Lord's hand was with them. The hand of the Lord signifies divine blessing and approval of the ministry of the believers.

5. The Jewish law is in the Bible and came from God. Jesus and his original disciples were all Jewish. From a Jewish point of view, Gentile customs were inseparable from their pagan background and so should be rejected. The Judaizers' view may seem strange to us if we're not Jewish, but Western missionaries did much the same thing in the nineteenth century when they wanted Africans to adopt Western clothing and culture in addition to Christian faith.

7. Peter affirmed that God, who knows their hearts and showed his acceptance in giving them the Holy Spirit, made no distinction between Jews and Gentiles. The latter received the Holy Spirit without being circumcised.

8. James said that the Jews should not make it difficult for the Gentiles to come to faith in God. He thought the Gentiles should abstain from certain practices associated with pagan religion (eating meat from butchers attached to pagan temples, etc.), although their salvation was not dependent upon these regulations. In observing these new stipulations, they were meeting Jewish believers halfway and enabling Jewish and Gentile believers to eat together without offending Jewish consciences. James believed their individual relationships with God would benefit as well.

10. The leaders in Jerusalem asked them to give up certain food practices from their culture that were especially disgusting to Jews, in order to make shared meals easier, but they didn't ask the Gentiles to completely reject their home cultures. On the whole, the Jewish believers made a huge leap forward in embracing the radical idea of Gentiles being acceptable to God.

Developing

12. If members of the group have committed to spending time alone with God, congratulate them and encourage them to take their commitment one step further and begin journaling. Review *Journaling 101* in the *Appendix* prior to your group meeting so that you are familiar with what it contains.

13. It's time to start thinking about what your group will do when you're finished with this study. Now is the time to ask how many people will be joining you so you can choose a study and have the books available when you meet for the next session.

Session Seven Prison Evangelism

Growing

In session 7, we will be covering Acts 20–26. Don't forget to remind the group to read these chapters ahead of time.

3. The gospel had spread widely among Jews in Jerusalem who were deeply attached to the law. When Paul traveled among Gentiles, he deliberately set aside Jewish food and purity laws in order to eat with non-Jews. Possibly other Jews in his missionary team did the same. This was good for evangelism among Gentiles, but bad for evangelism among Jews, who were offended that he treated the law as optional, not essential. James and the other leaders felt that a little public law-keeping would go a long way to keep the peace in Jerusalem.

138

4. Paul didn't believe keeping the Jewish law was wrong or spiritually harmful if one was doing it among Jews for the sake of the gospel. He just believed it was optional and therefore should be set aside when one was among Gentiles. Gentiles should not be given the impression that the gospel was "Jesus plus something else: Jewish culture."

5. Paul is accused of teaching against the law, the Jewish temple, and the Jewish people; and of bringing a Gentile into the temple. The charge about the Gentile is clearly false. From Paul's letters we know that he didn't teach against the law or the Jewish people. But teaching that the law was optional would have felt to a lot of Jews like teaching against the law. And teaching that Christ had fulfilled the sacrificial system implied that the temple (which existed for the daily sacrifices) was obsolete.

7. According to Roman law, a citizen was excluded from all degrading forms of punishment, including flogging. Torture was allowed to force a confession from an alien or slave, but not a Roman citizen (except under exceptional circumstances).

8. Pharisees (one of the parties represented in the Sanhedrin) believed that the righteous would be raised from the dead at the end of the age, while the Sadducees (the party to which most priests belonged) thought this belief was unscriptural.

9. Some of the Sadducee leaders made a pact to murder Paul. His nephew discovered it. Paul informed the Roman officer, and various Roman officials took action to transfer him to the Roman garrison at Caesarea on the coast for safekeeping. Luke is making a point of showing that the Roman officials did not think Paul had broken any Roman laws, and that the dispute was strictly a religious one. At the time Luke was writing Acts, the Romans were debating whether Christianity should be tolerated or outlawed under Roman law, whether Christians were a threat to society, so there was a good reason for Luke to lay out these early official opinions that Paul broke no Roman laws.

10. Probably Paul doubted he would receive a fair trial in Jerusalem, where people had plotted his murder. He had long aspired to proclaim the gospel in Rome (his letter to the Romans says this), he believed God was calling him to testify about Christ in Rome (23:11), and he wasn't afraid to do so as a prisoner under threat of death, if necessary.

11. Agrippa determined that Paul might have been set free had he not appealed to Caesar. Paul's appeal to Caesar had pretty much taken the matter out of the jurisdiction of Festus and Agrippa. Paul had to go to Rome. Though he could have been set free, Paul was instead on his way to Rome, where he would have the opportunity to proclaim the gospel.

Developing

14. Review the *Spiritual Gifts Inventory* with the group. Affirm those who have served the group or plugged into a ministry and encourage those who have not that it's never too late. If you have people still struggling with identifying their gifts, encourage them to talk to people who know them well. You might want to share what you've seen in them as well.

Sharing

15. Discuss the implication of Jesus's mandate to take the gospel to the ends of the earth on the lives of believers today. Have each person consider the action steps listed in this question and choose one to begin immediately as a way of doing their part in seeing this accomplished.

Session Eight To Rome and Beyond

Growing

3. In autumn, overcast skies made navigating by the stars almost impossible, and the threat of storms grew as winter approached. But the pilot and owner of the ship didn't think it was safe to keep the ship in the port of Lasea all winter, so they took a chance.

4. He means to reassure them, but he also means to make them curious about his God. Even in mortal danger, Paul is thinking about drawing people to Christ.

5. Paul tells the crew that they should eat to keep their strength up and that not one of them will be harmed. He offers God a prayer of thanks, and he eats with confidence that God is taking care of them all. He shows care for others and confidence in God that isn't shaken by danger.

6. There is no indication in Scripture as to why the centurion Julius wanted Paul's life spared. We can speculate that he saw God's power in Paul's life and so trusted him. We do know that as the highest ranking official on the ship, he could make this decision. The centurion's decision enabled Paul to continue his ministry in Rome and fulfilled Paul's prediction that all the people on the ship would be saved (27:22).

7. Paul is miraculously delivered from a snakebite and heals the father of Publius, the chief official of the island, as well as many others. The chief official, as well as many others, are affected by Paul's ministry.

8. The believers in Rome hear about Paul's impending arrival, and wanting to meet the great apostle, they travel south and meet his party at the Forum

on the Appian Way, a town about forty-three miles from Rome. A second welcoming group of Roman believers meet Paul at the Three Taverns, thirty-five miles south of Rome. Paul is sufficiently famous among believers, even in a city he has never visited, to warrant this hospitality. Paul sent his letter to the Romans several years earlier, so they know of him by that magnificent letter as well as by rumor.

9. Paul states his innocence of the charge of violating Jewish laws or customs. The Jewish leaders have not heard specific allegations about Paul, but they have heard negative comments about the Christians—and there is a growing group of them right there in Rome. So the Jewish leaders are interested to hear more about Paul's teaching. Paul persuades those whom he can. Saving his skin is secondary to sharing the gospel with any who will hear.

10. The response of these Jews replays a pattern that has continued throughout Acts: some respond positively, but most reject the gospel. Paul (citing Isa. 6:9–10) says that because of their stubborn resistance, he is turning to the Gentiles.

11. Paul remains under house arrest for another two years, during which time he writes the epistles to Ephesians, Philippians, Colossians, and Philemon. In Philippians 1 we learn that during this time the gospel continues to advance, and that even the Praetorian Guard, Caesar's elite troops, hear the gospel.

12. Luke ends the book of Acts by noting that Paul continues to proclaim the kingdom of God "boldly and without hindrance." The gospel of Jesus Christ cannot be chained. The theme throughout Acts is the unstoppable progress of the gospel.

Sharing

14. Allow one or two group members to share for a few minutes a testimony about how they helped someone connect in Christian community or shared Jesus with an unbelieving friend or relative.

DEEPENING
LIFE TOGETHER SERIES

Deepening Life Together is a series of Bible studies that offers small groups an opportunity to explore biblical subjects in several categories: books of the Bible (*Acts, Romans, John, Ephesians, Revelation*), theology (*Promises of God, Parables*), and spiritual disciplines (*Prayers of Jesus*).

A *Deepening Life Together* Video Teaching DVD companion is available for each study in the series. For each study session, the DVD contains a lesson taught by a master teacher backed by scholars giving their perspective on the subject.

Every study includes activities based on five biblical purposes of the church: Connecting, Growing, Developing, Sharing, and Surrendering. These studies will help your group deepen your walk with God while you discover what he has created you for and how you can turn his desires into an everyday reality in your lives. Experience the transformation firsthand as you begin deepening your life together.